BOUNDLESS

A ROADMAP TO A LIMITLESS FUTURE

by Kathy Eldon

AND HER NOISY SPIRITS

NOISY SPIRITS PRODUCTIONS

A Vital Quickening

"There is a vitality, a life force, a quickening that is translated through you into action, and there is only one of you in all time. This expression is unique, and if you block it, it will never exist through any other medium; and be lost. The world will not have it. It is not your business to determine how good it is, not how it compares with other expression. It is your business to keep it yours clearly and directly, to keep the channel open. You do not even have to believe in yourself or your work. You have to keep open and aware directly to the urges that motivate you. Keep the channel open. No artist is pleased. There is no satisfaction whatever at any time. There is only a queer, divine dissatisfaction, a blessed unrest that keeps us marching and makes us more alive than the others."

— Martha Graham

www.kathyeldon.com

Printed in the United States of America

First printing 2025

ISBN- 979-8-9929334-0-6
ISBN- 979-8-9929334-1-3

Noisy Spirits Productions
18820 Pacific Coast Highway, Suite 201
Malibu, CA 90265

Managing Editor: Alicia Dougherty
Creative Director: Tihane Mujić
Graphic Design: Hilary Rose Mix, Dawn Black
Editors: Andi Gitow and Rachel Warmath
Cover: Hilary Rose Mix, Tihane Mujić
Cover Illustration: Dan Eldon
Illustrations: Kathy Eldon
Back Cover Photo: Philip Alderton

Profits from the sale of this book will go to support
Creative Visions Foundation
www.creativevisions.org

This book is dedicated to the kids who inspire me,
Jack, Daniel and Arabella Turteltaub, Mac, Jimmy and
Mila Bedner, Indra and Bodhi Bedner, and to Amy Eldon
Turteltaub, Michael Bedner and the boundless Eva Haller,
Noisy Spirits who fuel me.

CONTENTS

BOUNDLESS
A ROADMAP TO A LIMITLESS FUTURE

Welcome to *Boundless,* an interactive collection of rhyming stories and prose reflections, whimsical drawings and thought-provoking questions that I hope will help you navigate the insanity of life's ups and downs. During a time of existential challenges in our world, let this little book encourage you to rediscover your purpose and embrace obstacles with an open heart and a courageous spirit.

Whether you seek inspiration, guidance, or a moment of joy, please consider *Boundless* as your traveling companion, reminding you that hope is always within reach and that together, we can create a brighter future. I hope that these musings from my Noisy Spirits and me will stir your soul, uplift YOUR spirits, and invite you to see and be in a brave and limitless way.

Boundless was born from the tumultuous times we live in—an era where the impact of accelerating climate change, unprecedented political upheavals and a mental health epidemic are challenging the very foundation of our shared existence. Across the globe, people of all races, religions, orientations and nationalities are searching for a sense of hope and direction, while grappling with fear and uncertainty. As I write these words, Los Angeles fires are raging, forever disrupting the world as we knew it when we were evacuated from our home. After three days of fighting the fires, our home and the building housing our treasured Creative Visions Foundation remain as two of only a few structures standing for nearly three miles along the Pacific Coast Highway. Although one day we will return (I have no idea when), we wonder how it will feel to live in the midst of such total devastation.

Staring at a future that seems more challenging than ever, I am determined to remain hopeful that we can and will respond to the myriad challenges we face in time to ensure that children around the planet can enjoy peaceful, positive lives. Sadly, many have already experienced anxiety resulting from the isolation they endured during the Covid Pandemic, a sense of unease exacerbated by the noise and chaos currently swirling around them. Youth are remarkably resilient, however. I was heartened last week, when, after three evacuations following the fires that destroyed my nine-year-old granddaughter Arabella's school and the town of Pacific Palisades, Arabella drew a green sprout topped with a bright red ladybug standing proudly against a brilliant blue sky.

While grappling with uncertainty about what's to come, I am grateful for whispers from an unseen source I affectionately call my "Noisy Spirits." These voices, full of whimsy, yet grounded in profound wisdom, have offered stories, often in rhyme, which have helped me navigate the struggles of my personal life and the wider world. As someone who had never written a poem before, I have been astonished by their unexpected transmissions, which display remarkable prescience and a belief in humans' ability to create a better world– if we pull together.

This book is my attempt to share their messages along with glimpses into my own journey. You'll find snippets from my memoir, *In the Heart of Life*, reflections co-written with my daughter, Amy, in our *Catcher* series of guided journals, as well as inspiration drawn from mentors, teachers, and guides—both visible and invisible—who have lit my path.

This book is also for your thoughts and dreams, a challenge to listen to your own Noisy Spirits, (or whatever you wish to call that source of inner guidance– God, Source, intuition, Spirit, Muses) who may have something important to say.

Please explore this collection with an open heart and mind, and fill the margins with your reflections and doodles that express your unique way of seeing and being in the world. I know that together we can find the courage, connections, and creativity to navigate these times with unbounded energy, and as much grace and joy as we can muster.

Enjoy the journey!

Kathy Eldon

NOISY SPIRITS

My relationship with "Noisy Spirits" began during the stillness of the Covid pandemic. At a time when the world seemed to come to a halt and uncertainty filled the air, something unexpected stirred within me. Rhyming stories and poems began to flow, uninvited but seemingly unstoppable, as if carried by a force beyond my control. I described the source as my Noisy Spirits, reflecting my belief that the words must come from disembodied entities that seemed to hover around me, full of advice and ideas if I was ever quiet enough to listen.

I had been vaguely aware of the presence of another dimension before the death of my son, Dan, an artist and Reuters photojournalist who was killed in Somalia at the age of 22 in 1993. But as a fact-based journalist, I needed proof that my son's spirit was communicating with me, even if I couldn't see him. Dan had been a noisy spirit as a seven-year-old, when my then husband Mike Eldon and I moved from London to Kenya with Dan and his little sister, three-year-old Amy. Inspired by the creative, hard-working individuals we met in that young African country, Dan learned how to seek solutions to the challenges faced by those in need. At the age of 21, Dan took photos for Reuters News Agency that ignited a global response to a horrific famine in Somalia, triggering an international aid mission, saving the lives of hundreds of thousands of people. Dan stayed on in Somalia for a year working as a Reuters photojournalist while the country spiraled into a bloody civil war. Tragically, on July 12th, 1993, Dan, together with three other journalists, was murdered by a mob in Mogadishu while trying to tell an important story.

Heartbroken, I wasn't sure that I could survive the pain of losing my son until my daughter Amy, then 19-years-old, and I decided to try to transform the horror of his death into a positive force for good. Strangely enough, it seemed that was a trigger for Dan's spirit to let us know he was still very present, as he offered thoughts and ideas about our work, whether we liked it or not. Sometimes, I felt Dan to be the ringleader of a motley crew of dearly departed souls determined to convince me that we can communicate with those who are no longer physically present–and that they may have something important to tell us. During Covid, the message came in the form of what I later learned is called "pop poetry," an unfamiliar medium for me. I suspected that one voice was that of a rapper, cut down in mid-verse, or Dr. Seuss, trapped in limbo, breaking free long enough to transmit messages to those of us who are uncertain how to navigate the unknown existence that lies ahead.

Recently this communication has grown even more urgent as we face the mounting challenges of our time: the frequency of unnatural disasters, massive political upheaval and increasing social division. But my Noisy Spirits insist that this is not the moment for despair but for deliberate, optimistic, and transformative action. They shout that we must embrace a new way of seeing and being–rooted in connection, courage, and creativity. Recently, during this time of intensifying global chaos, their messages have compelled me to seek new purpose, to find hope for connection amidst the discord, and to loudly share what I am learning in every way possible.

My Noisy Spirits still awaken me often, challenging me to believe in the possibility of boundless personal and global transformation and to use my/their/our words to help illuminate a path forward for myself and others.

CHAPTER 1

WAITING GAME–
THE POWER OF THE PAUSE

Life can be frustrating as it moves between rhythm and chaos—days of joyous soaring, scary sinking, and those strange in-between moments when simply existing feels overwhelming.

This chapter explores those inconvenient pauses, starting with inertia—when retreating under the covers feels easier than facing the day. Yet, within that stillness, the first spark of awareness flickers: the choice to rise or remain stuck. Overwhelm often follows, our minds tangled in too many worries, with too little control. But it's then that we must try to find comfort in small joys, in the simple anchors that tether us back to center.

Then there are the racing thoughts that won't allow us to rest, mind scurrying like a frightened mouse through what-ifs and worst-case scenarios. But over time, I have discovered that I can calm myself if I remember the concept of flow, seeing obstacles not as endings but as invitations to grow. Sometimes, I must step back entirely—choosing rest, letting go and embracing the wisdom of self-preservation. When decisions twist me in knots, I try to remind myself that clarity doesn't always come immediately and that choosing peace over drama, stepping away when needed, is its own kind of power.

Worst of all are the days when life grinds to a halt—when sickness forces me to surrender. Stripped to my simplest self, I grit my teeth and endure, trying to find humor in the waiting, lightness in the gloom.

This chapter is a journey through moments of retreat, of restlessness, resignation, and brave resistance. But threaded through each is an undercurrent of hope: that we will rebound. We will persist, and find our way through, even if we have no idea how. Even on the heaviest days, these moments are not destinations but, as much as we may hate them, they are necessary pauses—spaces to breathe, reflect, and remind ourselves that nothing will defeat us!

MORAL TORPOR

There are days when returning to bed with a pillow over my head is the only solution.

I feel lethargic,
dull, slow,
passive, inert,
weak, and low.

I'm slothful, sluggish,
shiftless, and sleepy,
indolent, irritated,
listless and weepy.
Moral torpor is the name of this mood,
caused by my apathetic attitude.
It's time to roll up my sleeves,
get off my backside,
shift gears, abandon my fears.
Sit up straight
and try to feel great!
No more indecision!
I must try to see all
that I can possibly be.

"Hey, steady on girl!"
I can hear a voice inside me say.
This all sounds like a lot of trouble–
WAY too much struggle.

Okay, I say.
I'll go back to bed,
put a pillow over my head,
and play dead.

YOUR TURN

These pages are designed to trigger your thoughts and ideas about moving from apathy to action. (Or not.) Write notes in the margins, start a new journal of ideas, or just think about the questions. (Or not.) Remember, there are no rules!

When did you last feel like retreating from the world?

What helped you to move forward, or what held you back?

DISCOMBOBULATED

Stressing about things I can't control gets me down.

The world has got me down.
I feel discombobulated, distressed,
disgruntled and depressed,
I'm not alright today!
I'm uptight and upset in every way.
Irritated, agitated, and downright aggravated.

What kind of complicated life have I created?
I need to simplify and say goodbye to all
that makes me crazy.
Get lazy. Take a break. Sleep till eight.
Meditate. Cogitate. Eliminate!
Act cheerfully, not tearfully.
fearlessly, not fearfully,
carefully, not carelessly.

What will it take for me not to be
grumpy and agitated
but gruntled and combobulated?
No bad news about politicians
or climate data from statisticians.
No conspiracy suspicions.
or diagnosticians' bird flu predictions.
Just give me reruns of *Fawlty Towers*,
and big bouquets of fragrant flowers.

I need a quiet place,
a simple space

where I can be free
to be that me
I would so like to be.

A WHISPER IN MY HEAD

Have you ever experienced what feels like a whisper in your head, soft but unrelenting?

"You should be writing," the voice says to me. "Speaking. Creating. The world is waiting."

I hear it, feel it tugging at the edges of my mind, pushing me to wake up and listen. But instead of rising, I sink deeper into whatever I can do that feels easier than answering the call.

The clash between the knowing and the doing is wildly frustrating. Inside, I am alive with ideas, aching to take shape. I imagine the words, the actions, the creations that could change something—anything. And yet, I stay still. Frozen, not only by fear but also by inertia.

"I'll do it later," I tell myself. "After a latte. After another episode of *Bad Sisters*. After a nap." But the truth is, the more I resist, the harder it is to move. The voices inside grow louder, more insistent, urging, pleading:

"Get up. This is important. Get off your backside and DO something that matters."

I want to listen. I want to act. But instead I try to silence the messages that I know will only grow louder tomorrow.

And so, I go back to bed, pretending I don't hear what waits there, just out of reach, as I drift into restless dreams of all that I am meant to do but can't yet find the courage to begin.

BRAIN RACE

Learning that the way to go is into FLOW

Heart racing, mind spacing,
It's 3 a.m., and I'm a mess,
worrying about all that's amiss
and thinking about what could
or should or would be
If only I were a far cleverer me.

Mind scurrying like a mouse
in a creaky house.
I'm quivering, shivering
No use staying in bed.
Instead, I'll get up,
knowing that the way to go
is into FLOW,
and that I won't just survive,
but thrive, aware
that obstacles are there to test me,
seeing that they will challenge
every aspect of my being.

So, instead of racing
toward an uncertain destination,
I must follow my intuition
and allow the fruition
of seeds of possibility in me.

PLAYING HOOKY

I have found that "bless and release" is the key
to inner peace, but it's often easier said than done.

Do you ever wake up and say,
sorry, but I'm not coming into life today,
I'm going to walk, okay, run away.
Find a safe space, a quiet place
to disappear, not for months or years.
Just for now, while I release my fears
about all that is happening (or not) to me.

I need time to just be,
to hide from the endless tide
of bad news and dread
and remind myself of what Bob Marley said,
that "everything's gonna be all alright,"
and that I can deal with what lurks in the night,
when worries keep me tossing, turning,
seemingly never ever learning
that "this too shall pass."
and that "bless and release"
is the key to inner peace.

I must know that my glass is "half full,"
not the other way around,
And that I SHALL REBOUND.

It will relieve my fears
If I believe that I have the courage
to change the things I can

and accept without being discouraged
what I can't control
and the wisdom to know my role.

I should never make the inference that
blockages are a hindrance
but instead, remember that persistence
may be the way to win the day.
I must recall Winston Churchill's intonation
as he spoke to the people of his troubled nation:
"Never give in. Never give in,
never, never, never, never..."

So, if you are ready to moan
about your inability to find stability
please know that there are several ways to go:
Persistence, resistance, or FLOW,
best achieved by heading back to bed
to clear your head while you repeat,
"Nothing will defeat me."
Convinced that you are invincible,
Pull up the covers and become invisible.

YOUR TURN

Writing and drawing in my journals helped me get through the worst periods of my life, times when I had no words for my feelings, but I could try to draw them. I have included my simple doodles in this book to encourage you to express your feelings through creative expression. Remember, no one is watching!

What does the phrase "bless and release" mean to you?

How could you apply it in your life?

CONUNDRUM

How to turn a definite no into a yes... or not.

So... would you?
I said.
Shaking her head,
she said,
"I would if I could,
and I know I should.
But no."

So, I said,
shaking MY head.
"If you know you could
and you know you should,
you won't?"

"Yes," she muttered,
"I mean, no..."
she spluttered,
"I mean know I should
and I know I could
but it's just not good
for me today.
So, NO WAY!"

The situation called for a mediation–
so, I tried a negotiation.
"If you know you would
and you know you could
and you know you should,
what would make you say YES?"

Tossing her head, she grimly said,
"I know I could, and I should—and I would,
but I am just not in the mood
and besides, I don't like your attitude!
So, no more talk. I'm going for a walk."
Then she popped on her hat,
and that was the end of that.

GAME PLAYING

I don't want to play today.

It's the same old game
we play day after day.
The voice in my mind
grumbles and groans,
mumbles and moans,
leaving me stressed.
Distressed.

Even in my sleep,
I can hear it say,
"You always.
You never.
Why don't you ever?"

In my dream I scream,
"GO AWAY!
LET ME BE!"
"No Way!" I can hear it say.
"I'm here to stay."

I awaken, brain brooding,
anger volcanic in its intensity,
as I fail miserably
to be a more peaceful me.

FLU BLUES

Look on the bright side... you could be dead.

Coughing, sneezing,
snorting, wheezing,
nose running.
stuffed up head,
half dead.
What's happening to me?
What sort of virus
could this possibly be?
Covid, flu, or RSV?

Temperature rising,
Joints aching,
heart racing,
chest tight,
I'm just not right.
Lungs filled,
body chilled.
This is not the me
I want to be.

I'm discouraged, destroyed,
useless and annoyed,
bleary, weary, and, well,
more than a little teary.

Can someone please give me
a Vitamin C infusion
so I can get out of this inhuman seclusion.
Until then, I'll just wait and see
reruns of *I Love Lucy* on TV.

LISTENING INSIDE

As much as I fight it, I know that whether I retreat under the covers or escape into distractions to silence the whispers of my unfulfilled potential, these moments of stillness are not signs of failure but invitations to listen inside.

When stress knots us into tangled loops of indecision, and our monkey brains refuse to be still, the answer is not always to push forward but to step back—into rest, into reflection, into the simple joys that anchor us. Sometimes, clarity arrives in surrender, in allowing ourselves to pause without guilt, to play hooky from the pressures of being perpetually "on."

Even when illness forces us into unwanted stillness, there is wisdom in waiting, finding humor in endurance, and lightness in the worst moments. These pauses remind us that I am not defined by our restlessness or resistance but by our ability to rise when the time is right. In the end, nothing will defeat us—not exhaustion, not uncertainty, not even the long nights of racing thoughts. The pause is not the end of the story; it is where the next chapter quietly begins.

CHAPTER 2

BREAKING FREE–DISCOVERING WHAT'S POSSIBLE

Life often wraps us in invisible boundaries—self-doubt, routines, and expectations—until we find ourselves longing for something more. This chapter is a reminder that while real limitations exist, we can still break free, reclaim inspiration, and reconnect with joy and purpose.

Sometimes, transformation requires surrender, falling before we rise with greater peace and focus. When inspiration dries up, the smallest shifts in perspective can reignite creativity, shaking off stagnation and daring us to fly again. As we quiet the external noise, we begin to hear the subtle whispers—intuitive nudges urging us toward boldness, creativity, and growth.

If we choose to look, we'll find signs all around us—synchronicities, symbols, and sometimes whimsical reminders that we're not alone. We discover that hope, too, is not something to seek outside ourselves, but a limitless force already within, waiting to be nurtured. Likewise, joy isn't something we wait for—it's something we create, an inner journey rather than a distant destination.

To move forward, we must release the endless loops of self-judgment and regret, clearing space for new possibilities. This requires courage—the willingness to speak up, act bravely, boldly, and lead with conviction, despite the fear of consequences. If not now, when? If we stay silent, who will rise?

Breaking free is an act of self-discovery and radical permission. This chapter invites you to listen within, release what binds you, embrace play, and follow what calls. Through these reflections, we uncover the joyful and limitless self that has been waiting to soar.

TAP IN THE SKY

Time to cut loose and play!

Why have my creative juices run dry?
My cosmic tap in the sky
has been reduced to a trickle,
leaving me in a pickle,
unable to draw, write,
or even scribble.

Although I know
it's inappropriate to quibble
over a lack of alien transmittal,
Why, say I, did the tap run dry
when I try to do everything right?
I'm in bed by eleven, up at seven.
I eat sensible meals,
low on carbs, sugar, and salt,
so, having a dull mind
shouldn't be my fault.
I play word games
to sharpen my thinking.
but then I blink, and my brain
goes all fuzzy again.

However, this morning
during my meditation
I had a revelation
when a little voice inside me
said, "Stop this prevarication
and get out of bed!"

Instead, I rolled over with a groan.
"Don't moan!"
the voice inside of me said,
"No more being a bore–
a total snore!
Wear something
you've never worn before
and go for coffee
in a different part of town.
No looking down
at your iPhone–
Look up and let your mind roam.

Better still, start a conversation
that will spark your imagination.
Wander around an unknown space
and book a trip to a wild new place.
Radically shift what you're doing and seeing,
alter all aspects of your predictable being.

Cut loose and play!
Go on a vacation.
Wait...you can't, you say?
Okay, okay...
Try a staycation
if you have to,
but pretend you're away.
Eat burritos for breakfast,
And latkes for lunch.
Sip lattes at Linner
and abandon all thoughts
of a healthy dinner
while you revel

in being a gastronomical sinner.
Once you have tried
this regime for a week
then we'll speak."

ONE WEEK LATER

Guess what,
It worked!
And as you can see
I'm a brand new me.
Now, if you're willing,
I can almost guarantee
what happened to me
will happen to you!
So, no more being blue
about a dry tap in the sky.
Strap on a helmet,
and get ready to fly!

NAUGHTY NUDGES

My Noisy Spirits are more than muses; they are partners, guides, and agitators. They push me to confront discomfort, embrace vulnerability, and believe in the power of words to break out of whatever boxes us in—and, once freed, to ignite positive change. Through them, I have learned that hope is not passive—it is boundlessly active, alive, and contagious. It is a force that can ripple outward when individuals rise, connect, and step into their power to shape the world they want.

I miss my Noisy Spirits'
ghostly whispers,
naughty nudges,
and ethereal touches
that inspire so much
of who and how I am.

My invisible entities
encourage me
to see things differently–
intriguing intersections
and cunning connections
I may have thought of
but a lot I've not.
Sadly, my team spirit
have flown away,
for far too long, I say.

Dear invisible friends,
please return to my brain
so I don't have to strain
to hear you again!

Maybe my Muses
left because they have no other way
to say that I should stay away
from the swirl and twirl
of my strife-filled life.
When I stop stressing
about what's depressing,
get quiet and listen inside,
the spirits return to my brain
and start to get noisy again.
Without distractions,
that lead to inaction,
they fuel me
with thoughts and ideas,
visions and dreams,
that let me see
the biggest me
I can possibly be!

When my spirits say,
Hey, it's time for us to go,
I mumble and grumble,
No, no! Don't go away!
I say, please stay.

My dear, they say
in their most reassuring way,
We are always near. Right here!
As close as on your shoulder,
whispering, "Be bolder, bolder."
So I try to smile
when they shout,

"Come on, what are you waiting for?
it's your time to soar!"

TIME TO SOAR

GOD WINKS

Seeing certain signs and symbols as meaningful can stir us up.

I love serendipity and synchronicity.
Like dreams that wake me up
and songs that shake me up.
Chance encounters
that leave me surprised.
Wide-eyed!

Some folks say angel numbers
are signs to stir us up.
Some favor fours,
while others are into twos or sevens.
My favorite is 11:11,
which they say,
has something to do with heaven.

A friend says a hummingbird
means her grandmother is near.
As for me, when I hear
a Bob Marley song,
I know my son Dan
is whispering in my ear.

Many say signs and symbols
are just coincidences,
but I'm inclined
to believe those incidents
and chance meetings
are wry, sly greetings

from invisible beings,
friends in high places,
and secret celestial spaces
where they easily view you and me.

I'm included to be with those
who think these happenings are God Winks
from spirits who have something important to say,
but instead of being somber,
choose to speak to us through play.
My invisible friends keep telling me
I don't need signs at all,
for they are as close as on my shoulder,
encouraging me to stand up, speak out,
BE BOLDER! BOLDER!

Whatever you believe,
You may be relieved to know
that those behind the winks
won't blink if you don't think
they're not real.

They'll just keep on appearing,
hoping we're seeing and hearing,
but cheering us even if we're not.

YOUR TURN

When was the last time you had a gut feeling, heard a nudge from your inner voice or noticed a "God Wink?"

What did it say?

What did you do?

GOT HOPE?

Emily Dickinson was right.

"Got any Hope today?"
I asked.
Shaking her head,
the shopkeeper said,
"I wish I could say yes –
but no.
We had a supply...
Oh, was it last July?
But since fall,
None at ALL.
Say, how about a dose of despair instead?
There's plenty in stock today."
"NO WAY!" I said, shaking my head.

"Got Hope?"
I asked in another shop.
"Nope." I heard a woman say.
"Hope seems to have gone away.
You'd better try again another day."
I visited Google,
Amazon, corner shops
and a dollar store,
but no one had Hope anymore.
Everywhere I went,
the answer was the same.
"Got Hope?" I said.
"Nope, not a glimmer nor even a shred."
It seemed that Hope was dead.
But despair – despair had spread.

Then, one day on my Facebook feed,
I heard Helena Bonham Carter read
a poem that went like this,
"Hope is a thing with feathers
that perches in the soul
and sings the song without the words
and never stops at all."

More than one hundred years ago,
Emily Dickinson seemed to know
that the place to look for Hope
is not outside but in, for the home
of the bird called Hope
lies deep within our souls,
and that little bird sings loudest
when times are toughest
and we feel our very roughest.

In moments of despair
when your spirit needs repair
listen inside where the Hope bird resides,
Then, when someone asks
If YOU have Hope,
nope is NOT your answer.
"Sure," you say, in an encouraging way.
"If you are quiet for not very long,
you'll hear the Hope bird's song."
So, when times are rough,
and you need to be tough,
remember that your feathered thing
will remind YOU how to sing.

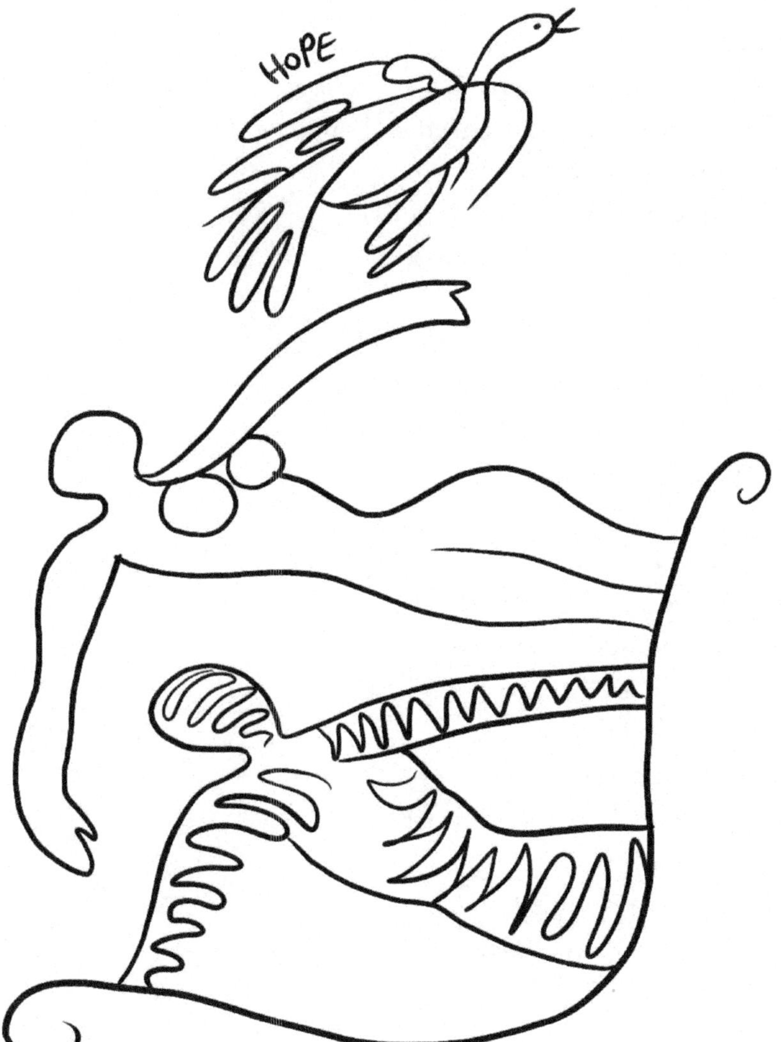
HOPE

JOY TRAIN

Sometimes, you just have to take matters into your own hands.

The other day, I read a sign
that said, "JOY TRAIN,"
but when I tried to buy a ticket,
the Ticketmaster shook his head and said,
"No tickets for this train.
Can't you see? It's supposed to rain!"
The next day I asked expectantly,
"Got any tickets for me?"
The guy looked me up and down and frowned,
"Sorry to be so bold," he muttered,
"But you are just a bit too old."
"NO WAY!" I spluttered.

A week later I returned,
"Have you got a ticket to Joy?"
I said in a high, squeaky voice.
"I'm hoping to go there to play!"
But when I tried to pay
I could hear the guy say,
"Can't you see? The train just left."
I felt bereft.
"I'll be back," I grumbled.
"Don't hurry," he mumbled.

Every time I went,
the answer was the same.
No tickets to be had,
though the reasons varied with the seasons.

"Can't you see?" The Ticketmaster growled,
"It's going to snow!"
"In this region?" I howled.
"I want to speak to the management!" .
"I'm the boss." he sighed."So I decide."

Bursting with indignation,
I was determined to get to my destination.
So, I rented a bike
and rode till the tires went flat.
Then I decided to hike.
The path, barely trodden
meandered through a forest
filled with ancient trees,
looming like silent guardians over me.
Through their branches
I could see snatches of clear blue sky
while below, autumn leaves lazily fluttered by.

When I sat down on the mossy ground
I breathed in air that smelled so sweet
I fell into a dreamless sleep.
Hours later, I awakened
to the rustle of a buzzing bee,
and the realization that
I had finally arrived at my destination.

"The Journey is the Destination"
Dan Eldon

LOOP ME

It's time to clear away the "shoulds, the coulds, and if only I woulds" from my mind.

Do you ever have words
that loop inside your brain
and repeat themselves
over and over and over again.
Mine are like a monologue or a soliloquy
about what I should've
would've or could've have said
to another who isn't me.

The words are very stubborn
and rarely go away,
although every morning
I wake up and say,
"NO MORE OF THESE WORDS TODAY!"
they still pop up in a most distressing way.

When thoughts unbound
swirl round and round,
instead of being present
in this time and space
I'm far away in another place.
I know it's time to shout those loopy words
at some convenient wall.
and figure out whether
they should be heard
by anyone else at all.
Maybe then I can clear some space

for thoughts that will take me
to a brand-new place
where I can bless and release
the shoulds, the coulds and
If only I would in my brain
so I can begin to live my life again.

YOUR TURN

What are the "shoulds, coulds, and if onlys" looping in your mind lately?

Write or draw what you're feeling.

TO HELL WITH THE CONSEQUENCES

If not now, then when? If not you...

I have thoughts inside my head
that demand to be said–
out loud, to a crowd.
For too long
they have been suppressed,
leaving me feeling repressed– depressed,
but today, my thoughts
demand to be expressed.

"No way,"
I hear a little voice
inside me say,
"Just think of the consequences!
You'll have no defenses.
You could be silenced
for what you say,
just leave it for another day."

And then I hear other
inside voices mumbling
and grumbling.
"If not now, then when?
If not you, then who?
The world is on fire-
we need people
who can inspire!"

"Someone else will do it better,"
I say, brushing them all away.

"We need a noble leader,
like Nelson Mandela,
or Martin Luther King.
or someone like Taylor Swift or Bono
whose gift it is to sing."

A charismatic leader
from an exotic place,
or maybe an alien
who descends from outer space!
A leader wearing sandals,
a leader wearing tatts,
or I know, how about lots of leaders
wearing funny hats–
like turbans or a crown?
Hey, we need all kinds of leaders,
leaders standing up,
and leaders sitting down!

We need women
like Oprah or Michelle.
Really, anyone who can sell
the idea that we are ONE.
that connection is the solution,
not shouting and dissolution."

"Today," I say, "We need
leaders who fight for unity and community,
instead of those who
divert us from democracy
to civil war and autocracy.
No more allowing the evolution
of an angry revolution!"

Now I can hear all my voices
shouting out loud,
as though to a crowd,
"If not now, then when?
If not me or you, then who?
it's time to take a stand,
and watch others stand up
to take a stand with you."

IF ONLY

If only I had more money...if only I had a relationship. If only I had a better relationship. If only my kids stopped fighting. If only I had kids. If only the world wasn't upside down. If only climate change wasn't ruining our lives. . . I would be happy. Sound familiar? I spent years believing that true happiness lay outside myself. Buried under the chaos and confusion of my daily life, I yearned for a respite from all that was happening. I ached for peace and the possibility of joy.

It took a total breakdown of all I had ever known and believed to discover that the essence of happiness comes not from what happens outside me, but how I am inside. It was an earth-shattering revelation, for I can no longer blame events, people or my upbringing for my lack of inner peace.

Think about those you know who seem happy. Chances are they aren't the ones with the perfect anything in their lives, except maybe their attitudes. However, these rare individuals have moved from being controlled by external events and influence to being able to remain calm, centered, and in balance, no matter what happens.

Bad things happen to us and to those we love. But despite all the things that rip into our lives, we have a choice-- to lash out, become self-destructive and hurt ourselves--or see the situation differently, roll with the punches and go with the flow, knowing that everything that happens is part of our growth. You don't have to be a guru or a saint to achieve inner peace. You do have to work at it, though.

Accepting life as it comes and trusting that we're okay, no matter what, demands learning to control our thoughts, so they don't run away with us. Wise teachers talk about living in the present, neither regretting the past nor anticipating the future. One way to do that is to follow a spiritual discipline to help you find your center and stay there. I'm terrible at staying still, but lately, I have tried to sit quietly and meditate or just listen to music or draw. It's then that the answers begin to flow.

It doesn't matter what you do if your mind and spirit have a chance to be alone with each other. It's in that union that you experience real peace and true joy. Despite the uncertainty surrounding you, choose to maintain harmony in your life as you take full responsibility for who you are and what you wish to contribute to our world. Radiate peace and joy wherever you go, knowing that what you give to others is what you will receive. These are difficult times to stay positive, but we will get through them, just as our ancestors managed to find their way through other challenging periods. We must "keep calm and carry on," as we work to manifest a vision of a fair, sustainable future for all.

KEEP CALM AND CARRY ON

CHAPTER 3

BECOMING–
FINDING YOUR COMPASS

My life is an endless quest to stay true to myself, as I strive to achieve my potential and lead the most purposeful, satisfying, and positive existence I can manage despite life's limitations. It's about finding my "bliss," as Joseph Campbell describes. It's about the sense of peace when we know we're on track, when we know who we are and what we are meant to do, don't let anyone derail us by telling us what we should think, feel, or do. We are the captains of our ships. We hold the compass.

But staying true to ourselves, especially during chaos and confusion, is the hardest thing in the world. So many voices are trying to make themselves heard, fingers pointing every which way. Then, we have to listen to our inner voices, to hear the wisdom of our higher selves, our intuition, God, Noisy Spirits, call it what you will. Let that wisdom show you the way. Listen. The voice inside you will tell you the truth–your truth. Learn to rely on your inner guidance, whether to help you create a master plan for your life or simply to get you through the next few minutes, days, or weeks.

Apply your boundless inner wisdom as you move toward that which lifts and energizes you, away from the limitations imposed by people or activities that drain your energy and take you down. Bravely follow your dream, no matter what anyone else says. For when you and your soul are headed in the same direction, the most incredible things happen. Even before the world finds balance again, be open to the magical, the mystical, and the inexplicable.

There is an old saying, "When the student is ready, the teacher appears." I have found that when we are truly committed, the opportunities, ideas, and people turn up at exactly the right time. Set your sights on your own star, keep your compass at hand, and bravely follow the boundless destiny you choose to create. And remember that "this too shall pass."

GRACE

Sometimes, we allow ourselves to be defined by labels attached to us in childhood, whether by well-meaning elders or unkind peers. Unless you are happy with them, ignore them. We are limitless. Unbounded. Infinite in our possibilities. And by the way, I am not clumsy. I just pretend to be to make people feel better around me. (Not true.)

As a child they called me Grace
to make light of a true disgrace,
for I was clumsy beyond belief
though I tried to turn
my dilemma into light relief.

Giggling and laughing,
I crashed into walls and tripped over air,
but always bounced back with nary a care.
Slipping and sliding I raced at a reckless pace
seemingly unaware of time, place or space.
One day I fell so hard I could not rise.
With no way to stand up that I could devise,
unable to will the power to get up and go
I finally had to let go.
Alone and desperate, sick of the race
I learned the true meaning of Grace.

Now on a new journey as a more peaceful me.
I strive to be more full of Grace,
Though still rarely ever grace-full.

A BOX CALLED ME

This poem was inspired by an exercise where you draw a box with nine smaller squares inside, each labeled with what occupies your life. In an ideal world, your box should include friends, jobs, children, and community activities, as well as time for yourself.

When I drew my box,
It seemed the square
meant for me was filled with air.
There were plenty of boxes for family and friends,
serving the poor, my job and more,
but mine looked like an empty drawer.

It seemed that others had grown and migrated,
while my square had shrunk and dissipated.
The box called me had ceased to be.
It's time, I declared,
that this situation is repaired.
I must show that I care not just about WE
but I also care about ME.

It's hard to get out of a cage at any age,
but when we make a belated effort to locate,
then deflate the outdated, antiquated expectations
that cause palpitations because they have expanded
beyond the boundaries that should surround us,
escaping may seem beyond belief,
so let me give you cause for relief.

For my part, I promise to make a brand-new start.
I'll try not to solve another person's problem

like the author of a Dear Abby column.
I'll learn a new way of seeing and being –
how to embrace another
without turning into his or her mother.
I'll get off my treadmill,
and learn to sit still, just chill,
allow goodwill to flow *in* as well as out.

I may soon doubt this solution
but if I make a firm resolution
there could be a revolution,
or an evolution in the space called me.
Perhaps a redistribution of the squares would help?
A substitution in one or two,
instead of what others
might view as a dangerous coup.

It's time to open the door!
Now watch me soar!
I'll start to write, take up kickboxing
and learn to fight.
Meditate with all my might.
Free my mind and remind myself–
no more strife in my life.

Oh dear, I can see the look on your face.
Please don't worry, I won't displace you,
my child or my brother!
I'd never abandon a friend or my mother.
I'll stick to my job, my service to others.
I'll only release what leaves me feeling diminished,
and work to complete the me that's unfinished.

Okay. I guess your reaction
means another plan of action.
I'll forget my crazy dreams.
Besides, all the squares are full again.
so I'll put my bold campaign on hold
until one day, I pray, before I'm too old,
I'll find a way to claim my space,
a place to be in and out of a box called Me.

YOUR TURN

In your box, how can you reclaim more space for what you need or want?

What labels or perceptions from childhood do you still carry today? Are they serving you or limiting you?

LET GO! You have so much inside you that yearns to be expressed. Please pull out the stops here and let it out!

I AM WOMAN

Many years ago, during a very difficult time, a dear friend helped create this mantra for me. I repeated it hundreds of times, often with tears streaming down my face. I still say the mantra out loud when I need to remind myself of who I am.

I am beautiful.
I am radiant.
I am loved.
I am woman

I am peaceful.
I am powerful,
I am prosperous.

I am strong.
I am capable.
~~I am in control~~ I am in the flow*

*I changed "in control" to " in the flow" when it became clear that I am in control of absolutely nothing, except how I react to people, situations and things I can't control.

RED LADY

As a young wife and mother, I traveled thousands of miles to Africa, where I first lost, then found, and then ultimately became true to myself. I have discovered an unexplored continent within each of us waiting to be found, a place of joy and sorrow, darkness and light, with limitless potential, challenging every aspect of our being. To respond to its call is to forever be transformed, for it is during this safari of a soul that we confront who we are and who we can become.

A thousand years ago or more,
I drew a red lady ready to soar.
Arms outstretched, naked and free,
Uncontained and unrestrained,
She was the me I always wanted to be.
But fearful and tearful,
masked and disguised,
I was a hollow shell in a self-imposed hell.

I realized that to become that me
I would have to find a new way to be.
I stopped crying and started relying
on my inner truth to show me the way.
It was ancient wisdom, though just as true now
that taught me how to release the bonds
I had created to hold me tight,
and discard the barriers
I had erected to keep out the light.
"Know thyself," intoned the Oracle of Delphi,
"to thine own self be true if you ever want to fly."
So, please release yourself from impossible demands
and begin creating your own new plans.

A thousand years ago or more
I embarked from a safe and familiar shore
and willed myself to soar.
Arms outstretched,
unconstrained and unrestrained.
No more fears and no more tears,
free to be forevermore me.

BRAVE NEW ME

It took decades before I followed the message of the Oracle of Delphi to "Know thyself." As I began to know and become true to myself, it became easier to tap into the never-ending source of love, power and energy that I believe connects and empowers us all.

Love, power, and energy
fuels my body, my mind, and my soul,
creating in me a brave new goal:
to fuel others with my energy,
sparking hope and love for all to see–
fulfilling my destiny to be courageously,
outrageously, joyously free
by finally being completely me.

LOVE
POWER
ENERGY

ACTIVATING YOUR SOUL

In the face of life's inevitable trials—whether a stifling job, a difficult relationship, financial strain, or an emotional crisis—we can feel the world conspire to hem us in, robbing us of hope, possibility, and our sense of freedom. Yet, within each of us lies an untamed capacity to transcend these constraints as the boundless, creative spirit that Ralph Waldo Emerson called "the active soul, free, sovereign, unencumbered." This soul, he observed, is our birthright but often remains "obstructed and as yet unborn," trapped beneath layers of fear, doubt, and external pressures. How, then, do we awaken this dormant part of ourselves and reclaim our boundlessness?

Visionary choreographer Martha Graham's words remind us of the profound power of the creative spark. To unleash this "unexpressed vitality," we must honor our creative impulses, even in our darkest hours. It is precisely in those moments of despair and restriction that creativity becomes a lifeline—a way to imagine new possibilities and break free of mental and emotional shackles.

But creativity alone is not enough. To embrace our full potential, we must also challenge the stories we tell ourselves about our limitations. Circumstances may seem immovable, but they are rarely the true barriers; often, the walls are within us, constructed from fear and self-doubt. The active soul Emerson described is not deterred by external conditions; it moves through them, growing stronger with each step.

To see ourselves as active souls, we must combine the courage to confront life's challenges with the willingness to imagine beyond them. We can begin with small acts: picking up a pen, a brush, or a new idea, reminding ourselves that freedom is not about perfect circumstances but the power to reclaim our inner sovereignty. In this brave way to see and be, we rediscover our birthright: a life unbound.

CHAPTER 4

LOVE LOST. LOVE FOUND–KEEPING LOVE ALIVE

If we are lucky, love weaves through our lives like a thread of unbreakable silk, stitching together moments of joy, pain, longing, and connection. This chapter is an exploration of love in its many guises—a journey that begins with the exhilarating, if weird, swipe of modern dating apps and meanders through the sometimes tender, often infuriating rhythms of lifelong partnerships, the seemingly boundless ache of loss, and the quiet persistence of memory.

Here, love wears many faces. It flirts and falters in the digital playground of Tinder. It deepens and strains under the weight of shared lives and growing families. It is tested in the fragmentation of those families and relationships but also transforms, finding ways to mend itself in unexpected companionships and rediscovered passions. Love looks backward, haunted by echoes of what was, even as it peers forward, daring to believe in new beginnings.

In this chapter, you'll experience the rollercoaster of modern matchmaking, and the sacrifices and humor needed to keep love alive in the chaos of family life.

You'll rediscover the magic of stolen moments, and learn how a broken heart might be the first step to healing.

As you journey deeper, you may be reminded of the bittersweet truths about the past—how it can shape, haunt, and occasionally surprise us. And finally, we confront the boundaries we must sometimes set, even with those we once held closest.

This is not just a chapter about love—it is a chapter about being human. For love, in all its tenderness, folly, and endurance, is perhaps the most human thing of all.

TINDER/TENDER

The absolutely frustrating pursuit of a mate in the time of social media

During a time of Tinder
whatever happened to being tender?
As in the lingering touch of a finger,
stroking a cheek or an arm,
a not-so-innocent gesture
meant to charm or disarm,
not alarm, like a mean screen swipe.

Left/right, right/left,
Now, quickly assess.
Is she/he more, or is he/she less?
Your decision is based on a guess.
He/she is an okay height,
But you say she/he's just not right.
I'd be inclined to sit tight,
better flight than fight

Left/right, right/left.
I'm getting stressed, really distressed
by this depressing quest.
Is there another way you could suggest?
You say flirt in a park, a gallery, or a bar?
Do people even do that anymore?
Feels like a bore. A chore. A total snore.
Left/right, right/left,
It's the big night.
A movie and out for a bite.
Mmm. . . is eye contact indicated?

Or is that concept outdated?
Should you hold his/her chair?
Gently brush back her/his hair?
Will it faze you if the other person pays?
Or was that just a feminist phase?

Later, at his/her place,
do you invade her/his space
and use his/her toothpaste?
then hug or snuggle, cuddle, or spoon?
Lie on the sofa and gaze at the moon.
Do you try to hook up?
Or just sit, iPhones in hand,
binging Netflix series on demand.
OMG, the next day
after coffee and toast
it could be over – cancel or ghost.
He/she/they could go totally silent
or obnoxiously boast.

Left/right, right/left,
losing tender to Tinder leaves me feeling bereft.
So what's he/she to do?
Hello Cupid, eHarmony,
Match, Hinge, Bumble or more.
You download the apps. I'll keep the score.

IN THE MOOD

Before you decide to grow your family, it's best to take a moment...

I lost me when we became three.
Before, when we were just two,
he and I, I was free to be...
well, for starters, alone when I pee.
Then we added another and soon, a baby brother
which meant quiet time was no longer mine.

Having company 24/7
made being alone feel like heaven.
Waking up in the night
to make sure the kids were alright
left me hazy, lazy and let's face it,
more than a little crazy.

There were other problems, too.
When I was a new mother
I sometimes tried to hide from my partner, my lover,
I hated to be rude,
but rarely was I in the mood,
and besides, when we started to snuggle,
I was turned off by his scratchy stubble.

Being married has joys we know,
but when your nuclear family starts to grow,
some of the glow is bound to go.
So slow down and enjoy each other
before you decide to create another.
Make love all night, then delight

in sleeping for as long as you like
or taking a hike without a crying tyke.
Extend your courtship and stabilize your relationship
before you add another, lose your grip and tip the ship.

If you have left it too late, don't despair,
for if you take enough antidepressants
you can survive your adolescents.
With luck, they'll leave home
and you'll find yourselves alone,
daydreaming about the way it used to be,
when the house was full and the fridge empty.
(No food, thanks to your insatiably hungry brood.)

Hey, with no distractions from the multitude,
a renewed attraction may put you in the mood.
So... turn out the lights and prepare to delight
in the pleasures ahead in the quiet of night.
Like sleep. Uninterrupted and deep.

PLAYDATE

Two perspectives on keeping the magic alive. Good luck.

Can we just stay in bed and play today?
When we're hungry, we'll run down the street
for a drink and a quick bite to eat.
Then we'll hurry back, crawl under the sheets,
tell Alexa to turn the volume down low
while we make love, above and below,
and bask in the afterglow.

Promise we'll always agree
to be romantic—carefree!
Say that you'll never outgrow me
and I'll do the same.
We'll never blame each other
but cherish one another,
give and forgive, as long as we both will live.

Three months later. . .

Darling, could you hand me the remote?
What? You won't change the channel until we vote?
That makes me unhappy and out of sorts,
sick to death of your constant sports.
I want to watch the Hallmark channel,
Anderson Cooper and a CNN panel.
I'll scream if I have to see your wretched team
score another goal at the Super Bowl.
You're totally out of control!

You, on the other hand,
can hardly moan about me.
You're always on the phone
in that confidential tone
that feels like a no go zone.
You drone on about how I should reveal what I feel.
Well, I would if we could have a conversation
about sports, movies, or the state of the nation.
Hey, let's stop all this talk
and go for a walk around the block.
Let's take stock and remember the promises
we made to one another
to love and cherish each other.

Sorry, if I sound rude,
but I am just not in the mood.
The laundry needs folding,
the dishwasher loading.
A Zoom call looms,
my boss is on hold
and if truth be told,
there's no freaking way
I can get away and play.
You will have to try another day.

YOUR TURN

How have relationships shifted for you during major life changes like marriage, becoming a parent, or losing a partner?

How can you reclaim aspects of you that you may have lost over time?

HEART. CRACKED. OPEN.

One way to heal a broken heart.

Never be reckless with someone else's heart,
he said, just before we parted,
or rather, he departed,
leaving me in uncharted waters
without a rudder or even a boat
to cruise around the moat
that encircled the castle
that guarded his heart.

Although I splashed and flailed,
I failed to scale the stone walls
guarding the inner halls
where he stayed, ready to prey
on another like me.
Someone eager to be loved like no other
until there was another.

Heart. Cracked. Open. Totally broken,
I cried until something inside me died.
So when he called to say,
Hey, how are you doing?
I replied. You are dead to me.
Suddenly, I felt free, oblivious to his plea
that the latest other was no more.
Out the door.

Later I found her floating in the moat
so I took her home, dried her tears

and soothed her fears.
Together, we clinked glasses,
"Cheers," we said, downing our beers.

LOVE LOST, LOVE FOUND, SORT OF...

For those who have memories of an old love rattling around in your head and heart...and really, who doesn't?

Did you ever try to relocate an ex
who refuses to vacate your mind,
even though you meant to leave them behind.
Is there a box tucked under your bed
filled with letters frequently read,
loving words stuck in your head,
though the one who wrote them to you
is to you, or so you said, dead.

Have you ever been to a class reunion
seeking reunion with an old heartthrob,
one you can't seem to release
even though if one of you doesn't let go,
you'll never be at peace.

Did you ever want to see,
or better still, BE with one you once loved but lost?
Spend a day, say, to allay feelings
that can still have you reeling,
though best not to spend the night
if you don't want to trigger fight or flight.
That will only complicate your plight.
Do you feel aching, burning, yearning,
or a piercing pain that leaves you
pondering, wondering, worrying
about how, when, or whether
you two will ever be together–
for a moment or forever?

Here is what you should do.
Replace the partner of your illusion
with a new one with no delusion
firmly planted in the here and now.
No more scheming or dreaming
about a fuzzy future when, if or how.

With your new love
be careful not to share unbidden your ex's name,
for you may reveal hidden feelings
best kept concealed about your former flame.
Remember, incendiary sparks once set alight,
may ignite pale embers, which fanned till bright,
could implode and explode into a wild wildfire
that, if not quickly restrained,
will be impossible to contain.

So, stay in the present.
Consider your partner a gift
and avoid doing anything stupid
that could create a rift.
Celebrate life, avoid strife
and delight in the dazzling light
that surrounds this beloved other,
who, one day, I pray
will not join the ranks of discarded lovers
whose letters you read under the covers,
the mere glimpse of whom sets your heart a throb,
with memories of nights that threaten to rob
you of much-needed sleep.
So please, when you want to weep about the past,
just bloody well make this latest lover last.

HOW DO I LOVE YOU?

The Greeks figured it out all those years ago.

Have you ever thought how absurd
it is that in English, we have only one word
to describe how you love your fiancé,
the songs of Beyonce,
blueberry pancakes,
or chocolate ice cream shakes?
Clearly, we don't feel the same
so we need another name
to reveal how to revere our wife,
our lover or our mother,
as opposed to a mountain hike,
a grilled cheese sandwich
or a new electric bike.

Ancient Greeks solved the problem with a love words list.
Six varieties are known to exist.
The first is *Philia,* describing how we care about
a comrade, a sister, or our brother.

Eros is the passion you feel for a special other,
a wild, uncontrolled love that will drive you mad,
before, during, and after an addictive relationship goes bad.

Agape is universal, selfless love we share with each other, full of
empathy and compassion as we look after one another.

We all need more *Ludus*–playful fun, laughing, flirting,
light romancing or even a night of tango dancing.

It's always time for *Philautia*–love of self,
e.g. never having to explain,
blame, forget, or lose oneself.

We should all commit to *Pragma*, a brave endeavor,
committing to a relationship meant to last forever.
(Not falling head over heels, but *standing* in love
so that even though you're mad at your husband
or wife, you don't pack up and leave your life.)

We can learn lots about love from those old Greek sages,
whose wisdom has lasted over the ages.

Like avoid too much *Eros* if you don't want a broken heart
(Which is most likely when you and your crazy lover part.)

Instead, cultivate *Philia* with a trustworthy friend,
knowing that this deep connection need never end,

Then enjoy *Ludus,* dinner, and a late-night dance,
without feeling the need for crazy romance.

Work with your *Pragma* partner to release
feelings that don't increase
a sense of deep and lasting peace.
But most important of all,
learn to love YOU and to thine own Self be true.

Then spread *Agape* wherever you go
because as the Greeks knew, and now you know
our world will be a far better place,
if you and I and all of us are in
a more joyous, peaceful and loving space.

THE KEY

Big lesson: when someone moves out, always get your keys back.

I gave away
the key to me
when I thought
he and I were we,
but that night we fought
and fought for nearly a year
until it was clear
that we were not meant to be.

After he departed
I fell apart.
My heart cracked open.
I was totally broken.
Oh, and the day
he went away
I forgot to say,
"Hey, before you go,
leave the key with me.."
So naturally, I was taken aback
when he came back
and once more used the key
to open my door.

I should have said,
"No. Go away!"
But instead, I said, "okay?"
That night, we fought and fought
till it was clear

that he and I still were not
meant to be.

But when we parted,
my heart didn't fall apart.
I was okay in every way,
except I knew he had kept the key.
So, I changed the lock on the door
and now he can't get into me anymore.

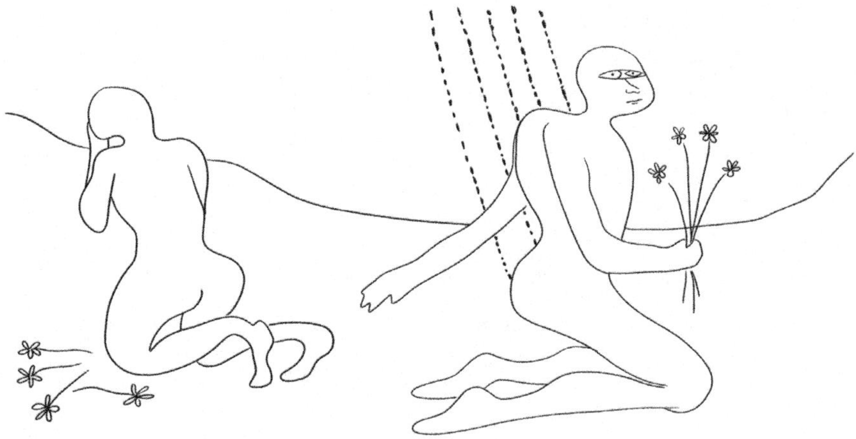

YOUR TURN

What emotional or physical "keys" have you given away in past relationships?

Write a letter of release to someone who has hurt you. What will you say to set yourself free?

SECRET SPACE

Remembering the ache.

Once, I fell for a dangerous man,
seduced by his charm
and his taste and his smell.
Meeting you sent me
back to the days
when I ached to fly
escape, disappear – soar high.
Ensorcelled, entranced,
entertained and romanced,
It took your gaze to see
how I could once more
be that untethered me.

Now I'm in my secret space,
a place of possibilities.
Before I return to normality,
I want to savor this reality,
allowing the creation
(if only in my imagination)
of that new/old way to be
if I could allow myself to be that free.

But here's my fear,
that you will not find
what's in your mind
when it is truly ME you see.
Still, if you are game,
we can find each other again-

though perhaps more wisely,
we should stay in blissful un-reality.

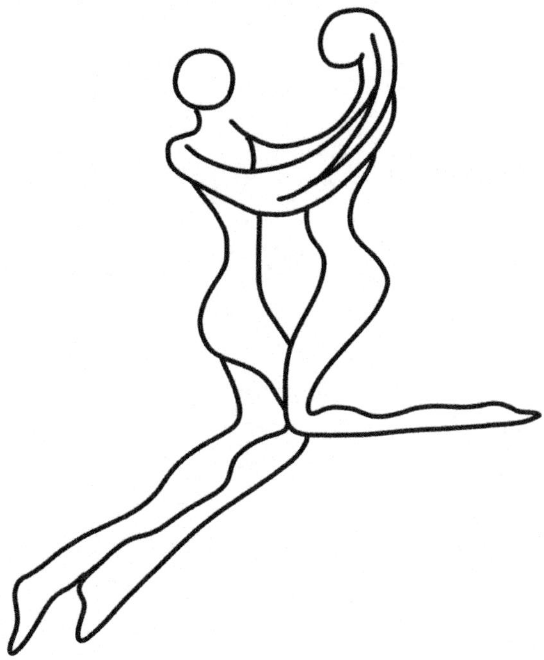

DEFROSTED

"It's life's illusions I recall..." Joni Mitchell

Mesmerized and magnetized
by memories of a long-ago union
in a faraway place,
a vision frozen across time and space.
I decided to find what was in my mind,
a reunion with he who had so deeply
imprinted that image on me.

It took years till I found the one
I had long been longing for,
but when I opened the door,
I watched in horror
as that frigid vision
melted into a puddle on the floor.
As I left, I wept for a lifetime of delusion
seeking an illusion.
But then, outside in the half-light
of approaching night
I saw a man waiting at the gate.

Sorry, I'm late, he said
in a voice so low
I could hardly hear
when he spoke my name.
He looked familiar
but I couldn't quite place him.
His face was broader,
his body too.

But when drew me
into a warm embrace, I knew.

"I thought I had lost you,"
we said as one.
Indeed, I had lost him
and he had lost me, too.
But then we walked and talked
and talked some more
until we were no longer sad but glad
that the defrosted illusion
had dispelled our delusion,
so now we could see
how or even whether
we were ever meant to be.

LOVING YOU. LOVING ME.

We all want more love in our lives, but often, we don't know where to find it. Some of us long for romance with a real companion to give us more than a virtual hug. Many yearn for the rebirth of an old relationship or need guidance to help separate from a longtime companion. We want quality time with our children, the little ones who Zoom-bomb our meetings, and the bigger ones, phones in hand, who ache for true connection with their friends. We want to nurture far-away parents, and find new ways to be good friends and family members across the globe.

Many of us want more love in our lives, but often we don't know where to find it. We don't realize that to receive love, we must give it, not only to others, but to ourselves. We don't have to rely on anyone else, for inside each one of us is an infinite source of loving energy. We just have to open the tap and let it flow. It is then that we discover love is everywhere. Love is in the infinite mysteries of nature and the miracle of simply being alive. Love is in an unexpected email from a faraway friend and in momentary encounters with a stranger, whose eyes connect with ours. We can give and receive love in a gesture, a silent prayer, meditation, a gift of appreciation, or in an unexpected phone call. Give love away and you'll find it pouring back.

CHAPTER 5

LIFE. DEATH. LIFE– NO ENDING, NO BEGINNING.

Death. A scary word for many. Yet, beneath its shroud lies a paradox—an ending, yes, but also, perhaps, a beginning. The great unknown invites us and teases our imagination with dreams of liberation or reunification, even as it leaves us gasping for answers. Thinking about our mortality reminds us to live fully in the present, to cherish those we love and to live the life of our choice, now, not in some distant, uncertain time in the future.

In this chapter, we dance with death—not as an enemy to be feared, but as a companion to be understood. We'll explore the agony of seemingly endless grief that hollows us, the boundless despair that drives some to prematurely embrace the void, and the relentless march of time that bids us to confront the limitations of our aging bodies and faltering minds. We'll also turn our eyes to the enduring essence of spirit, the ineffable hum of presence that lingers beyond the reach of our senses.

This chapter is an exploration of endings that may not be endings at all–but a recognition of those who leave us with a "you-shaped hole" in our hearts yet somehow remain–a match in the darkness, a nudge of courage when we falter, a God Wink that whispers in the stillness. It is a plea for us to consider, even as we grieve, that love transcends, spirits endure, and the noisy energy of life carries on, eternally reshaping itself.

These poems are not merely about loss but about the possibility of continuity. They are tributes to the loved ones who have left us yet refuse to leave. They remind us to live boldly–now– to say the unsaid, to forgive the unforgiven, and to seize this precious, fleeting gift of life, while being aware that death may be but a blink as our boundless spirits find new wings to soar.

"Death is just a horizon, and a horizon is only the extent of our view."

Dan Eldon

WHERE DO WE GO WHEN WE DIE?

This is an homage to the Dead Parrot Sketch. If you don't know about it, please watch "Monty Python" tonight.

Where do we go when we die?
Do we graduate life and fly,
tassels twirling in the sky?
Do we soar in blinding light
or lie in unending night,
contemplating each mortal sin
with nary a heavenly violin.
How will we be when we pass away?
Will we yearn for a return to the earthly fray,
or eager to make ethereal hay?

I'd like to think that all of us
quickly shed the annoying fuss.
Liberated at last from human pain,
no more hurt, no more blame.
Uncontained and unrestrained,
without the demeanor we once maintained,
now doing as we please.
(No more waiting till another agrees.)
Seeking the spirits we loved and lost,
ignoring those we blithely tossed,
we unite with souls once adored,
hearts as one, our love restored.

What happens after we are extinct,
when we have ceased to be?
Here is what I'd like to think.

When I am bereft of life
and have left behind all earthly strife
my spirit will be a noisy one
demanding others join the fun
I am planning a forever vacation,
a rest first, then re-incarnation?

"There is no ending, no beginning,
only the infinite passion of life."

Federico Fellini

BLINK

A reminder to live fully, love much, and try to leave the world a better place because you were in it. (Thank you Ralph Waldo Emerson.)

When you're young you never think
life could be over in a blink.
But then your mileage gauge ticks faster,
leading you to the ultimate disaster.

When days, months, and even years
fly by filled with joy and tears,
You realize your mortality
and that one day
you, too, will be a fatality.

Instead of being fearful,
I choose to remain relentlessly cheerful
and die from too much giggling.
Wriggling with delight in the fading light,
blissfully unaware of my plight,
I will slip gently into eternal night.

A FINAL THOUGHT

Hunter Thompson once said, "Life is not a journey to the grave with the intention of arriving safely in a well-preserved body, but rather to skid in broadside, thoroughly used up, worn out, and loudly proclaiming,

'Wow, what a ride!'"

YOUR TURN

This may have been a tough chapter for those who prefer not to think about what's ahead for all of us. Still, no matter how old or young you are, please be kind to those who will have to deal with things after you depart and make sure someone knows the passwords to anything that needs to be accessed. Your survivors will love you more for it.

How do you feel about the idea of life after death? Hopeful, fearful, curious, or something else?

How can you transform the pain of grief into a force for good?

PHANTOM LIMB

In this poem, I recall how I felt the first year after my son Dan's death.

I don't have words to express the grief I feel,
the look in my eyes should be enough to reveal
the ache in my heart and how close I am to falling apart.
It has been a year, but as with a phantom limb
that hurts, although it is not there,
I remain in indescribable pain.

Since you passed, 365 days have passed.
There is a belief that by now
I should have found some relief.
But if asked, I would say
that my grief will never go away.
I want to be wrong,
but right now, I would happily die
if it meant I would never again cry
for he who I loved beyond measure.

The memory of the one whom I so treasured
lies buried in my heart
though his soul has long departed.
Hawk-free, wheeling sky high,
he has learned to fly,
dipping, diving, riding currents of air
up there, somewhere.
Not fair, I say, for his spirit to so freely play
while mine remains earthbound,
planted on hard and unyielding ground.
When I ask, can my soul join his?

Free of the need to be a solid me,
while he, ephemeral, ethereal, invisible,
can with childlike joy and infinite grace
eternally soar across time and space

When I finally ascend, I intend to transcend
all that has been holding me down.
Shedding trappings,
I'll head toward the sky,
determined to fly just as high.
Spirit soaring, pain released
I will finally find true peace.

After Dan was killed at the age of 22, I was determined to live as fully as possible. However, over the years, I forgot and took life for granted. The Pandemic reminded me of the imminent possibility of grave illness or death– and, for a moment, heightened my awareness of the importance of living fully and loving as much as possible. The LA Fires that devastated my community were another sobering reminder of the ephemerality of all that we hold dear. Once again, I must remember to express my gratitude to those I love. Tomorrow may be too late.

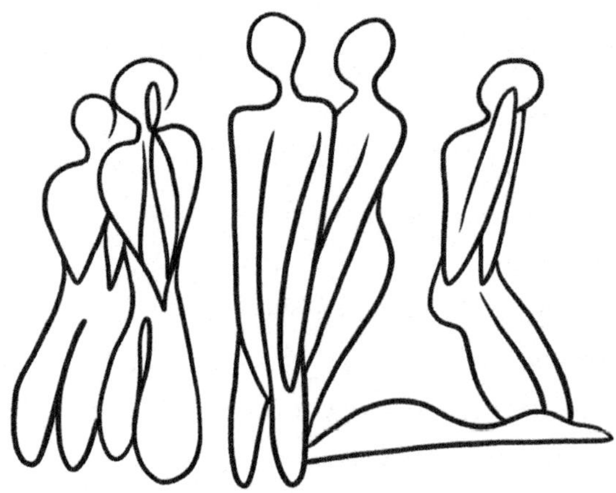

HOLE IN MY SOUL

The sudden tragic death of a young friend reminded me how important it is to reach out to those who may be suffering in silence- before it's too late.

When you left
I was left with a
you-shaped hole
in my soul,
a space I will never be able to fill,
because you, you see,
are irreplaceable to me.

My heart aches; no, it breaks
when I think of a world without you in it.
Just three days before you left,
we walked and talked about all
you were planning to do and see
as the new you you were trying so hard to be.
We spoke about kids, films, books, and friends,
so not for a minute did I think those conversations
would mark the end and that
so suddenly you would be leaving us
despairing and grieving.

Were those brave smiles just make-believe
to make me believe that all was well,
and that you had finally filled the hole in your soul,
the one you once you described as an empty shell,
a lonely, living hell.
I should have known something wasn't right

for as we said goodbye that last night,
your tears began to flow,
and my anxiety began to grow
when I saw your fragile spirit
begin to crack, then break
with the pain of what seemed
like an unbearable heartache.

But then we talked some more
and all seemed well before
before we parted at the door.
Then you departed,
heading now I know
toward some distant, unknown,
and unknowable shore.

Please know I will cherish you always,
though now with a you-shaped hole in my soul
a space I will never be able to fill, for,
you see, you are irreplaceable to me.

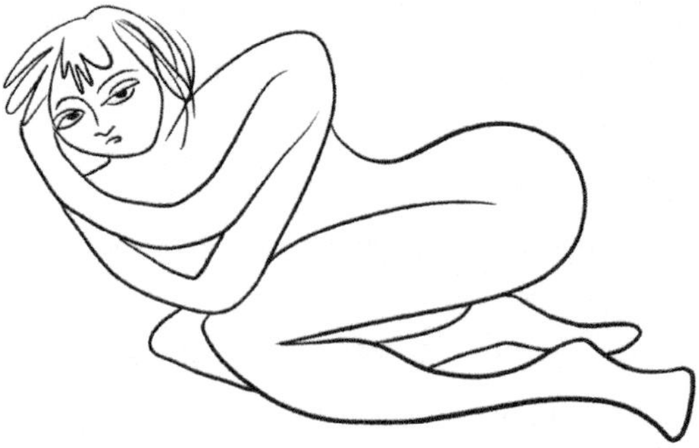

FINDING WINGS TO FLY

For my daughter Amy, who has always encouraged me to stop flapping, have faith and soar.

Dearest Amy Louise,

I promise you that I will not undo this demand,
so please consider it a loving command.
When I'm unwell and past my sell-by date,
I would hate for you to try to hold on to me
for I want to go with grace and dignity.
So may I enlist you to assist
when it's time for me to cease to exist?

Don't resist, my beloved daughter,
for you are not leading me to the slaughter
but only fulfilling my request to do
what I believe is best for me and you.
You see, I never want to forget your name
or do anything that would make you feel ashamed.
so, this is how I would like to depart.

First, we will sip some Yorkshire Gold tea,
with honey for you but none for me,
Next, please take me for an airplane ride
dipping and diving in a clear blue sky,
Then, when it's time, not a minute before,
open the door, push me out,
and watch me soar!

You know how long I have flapped,
when I really wanted to fly.

So please don't cry as I take flight
heading towards a brilliant light
Don't be sad, my darling Amy.
but glad that I am free,
and that we will be reunited
through all eternity.

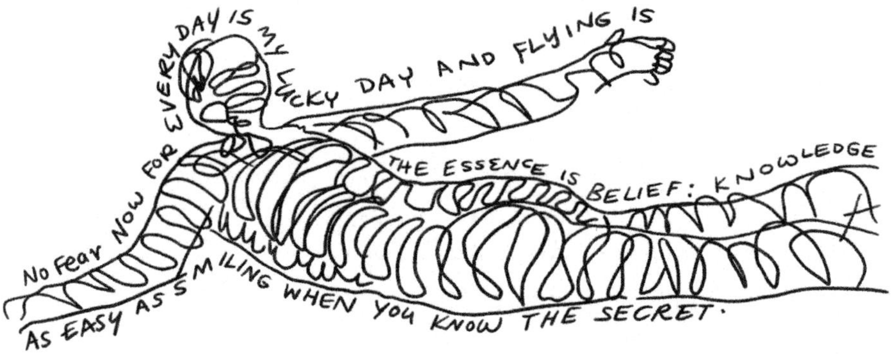

NOISY SPIRIT

As a former journalist, I look for proof. Proving the existence of life after life isn't easy, but my experiences with my invisible Team of Spirits have convinced me of the enduring life of the human spirit.

Twenty years ago, or more
My son Dan departed for some distant shore.
But I don't believe that anymore,
for if he has gone that far,
why do I feel him around me
almost every day,
smiling in his inimitable way
(Mostly in the half-light of approaching night,
then gone if I look too closely.)

Sometimes I see him in my dreams.
It seems he appears when
I'm most anxious and concerned.
Then he stands above me, looking down,
with a tiny frown as though to say,
remember, I'm never far away,
and one way or another
as Bob Marley always said,
Everything's gonna' be alright.
Things'll look better in the morning light.

Other times, I feel him on my shoulder,
encouraging me to speak up.
Be bolder. Bolder.
He says that I must not doubt his existence,
for there is no distance between us.
I must ask for assistance, though,

for spirits aren't meant to appear to interfere.
So, Dan, I'm asking you how we can
heal our ailing planet because
we didn't plan it to turn out this way.

I know what you'll say.
We're beyond remiss in what we've done,
but please don't dismiss this plea
for we urgently need help
to ignite the change we wish to see,
the one Gandhi said we each must be.

So, Dan, can you please bring your man
Mahatma to an emergency meeting?
I'll organize the seating.
Hey, while you're inviting,
Could you set up an RBG sighting?
Let's include Martin Luther King,
Bobby Kennedy and his brother,
my father and my mother,
and any others who can be of service
because I'm super nervous
that we have left this all too late,

I hate to think that our world could be finished,
our seas polluted; our crops diminished
because we haven't heeded
the wise beings who preceded us,
Like Chief Seattle, who declared
that air shares its spirit with all the life it supports.

That day, he exhorted in his powerful way
that the earth does not belong to man.

Who then? I say.
Man belongs to the earth, he said.
And all things are connected.
It's a concept we have long rejected.

So, now, can we recall Chief Seattle's words
and act to forestall the doom and gloom that lie ahead?
Just imagine. If we unite to fight planetary blight,
we can start to set things right--head towards the light.
Connected to one another, to Spirit, and to our land,
we can create a bright new future for humankind.

Instead of grief, pain, and sorrow,
we can ensure a kind, loving, and equitable tomorrow.

CARPE BLOODY DIEM

A reminder to reach out to the one you know needs to know that you care. Today.

I could hear words
inside my head,
words that felt important,
like portents
of things to come.
But I was sleepy and
couldn't find a pen,
so instead I said
I'd remember them.

Around three in the morning,
I woke up with what felt like a warning,
a rap on the wrist,
a reminder
to recall what
I might have missed.

When it was light
the words I had heard
so clearly that night
had, like morning dew,
evaporated, disappeared,
been erased, vanished without a trace.
Inside my head,
I heard a voice say,
"We have an important message for you,
but you blew it... so here's a clue."
Then I recalled two words from all those that

had taken flight that night.
Carpe Diem, Seize the Day.
I heard the voice inside me say.
Today, reach out to the one
who needs to know
how much you care,
and share what you know
would matter most
with the one who most matters.

Start with what's easy,
Like, I'm sorry
I made you worry,
Then you could say,
please forgive me.
for what I have done
or still might do that may have
or could hurt you.

Then pause.
It's a lot to take in.
Then begin again
and mean it
when you say,
Today, I forgive you, too.
Then just be still,
because you will want to hear
words you might fear
that he/she/they could say,
words that would reveal
pain in private places
and secret spaces about wounds
that still may need to heal.

The next three words
could be the hardest
of all for you to say.
so, practice before you call,
as the words "I love you"
are the most important
words of all.

Carpe Diem!
Seize TODAY.

YOUR TURN

Think about a time when you "seized the day." What prompted you to act, and how did it impact your life?

Is there someone you could/should contact before it's too late?

Or a letter you want to write to someone you've lost—expressing what you couldn't say while they were alive?

JOURNEY OF SOULS

Michael Newton's book "Journey of Souls: Case Studies of Life Between Lives" inspired this poem. Newton's book affirms that our existence is not limited to the boundaries of our physical beings. I received the book from a dear friend, who died two months later. When I read the book after his passing, I realized why he had been so determined to give it to me.

If you find yourself apart
from the one who holds
the key to your heart,
your sense of desolation
may find consolation
if you know that certain souls,
destined to live, learn, and grow together,
will never truly part,
for they will remain forever a part of each other,
whether in this life or in another.

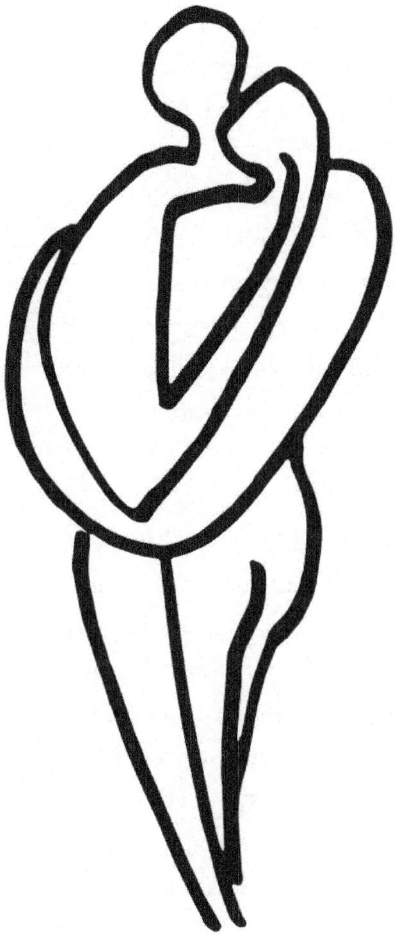

MEETING RALPH WALDO EMERSON

Millions around the world are grappling with the loss of a loved one, awakening every morning with a gaping hole in their hearts. As they grieve, they wonder whether they will ever be happy again. Knowing that life is precious and ephemeral reminds us to be aware of the gift that each day offers to us; another chance to love more, give more and express how we feel to those we love before it's too late.

After Dan was killed, Amy lived below me in a condo in West Hollywood. When she was upset with me (which happened quite often) she would stomp down the steps, slam the door, then crack it open while shouting, "I LOVE YOU!" This broke the ice, made me smile and usually sorted out the problem, for we both knew that any moment could be our last and we didn't want the final words between us to be unkind.

Those early years were extremely hard for both of us. It was only by transforming the pain of Dan's loss into a force for good that we were able to go beyond merely surviving and find ways to feel joyous again. It helped that I felt Dan's presence around me as a mischievous spirit who knew what I was up to and wanted to help. I was uncertain whether I should tell others about my belief in my ability to communicate with those no longer physically present, but I have learned that my experiences with my unseen guides and mentors mirror those of countless others who, like me, often feel too embarrassed to share them.

A few months after Dan's death, Amy and I discovered an electric typewriter that held within its memory his college essays. When we turned the machine on, it began typing a whimsical story about how Dan had run into the poet Ralph Waldo Emerson (then a sprightly 185 years of age) in a seedy bar in South Central Los Angeles. Dan described in detail his leather jacket, with the words, "The Great American Scholar," written on the back, and how Ralph took them on a wild motorcycle ride to the stacks in UCLA.

Seeing the students, barely awake over their books, Ralph laboriously crawled onto a table where he harangued them about the importance of learning. As they began to sit up and listen, he boomed, "The one thing in the world, of value, is the active soul. This every man is entitled to; this every man contains within him, although, in almost all men, obstructed, and as yet unborn." As Dan's words appeared on the paper before us, as though typed by invisible hands, the concept of the "active soul" awakened something deep inside me. I wanted my spirit to be fully activated, unobstructed and reborn, able to fulfill my highest potential, both for myself and for our world.

It's a wish I would have for each one of you —an idea that I hope will fuel you during these challenging times. As you allow yourself to be true to yourself, you will inspire those around you to activate their souls and begin to live more fully, love more deeply and to leave the world a better place because they have lived.

"What is success? To laugh often and much; to win the respect of intelligent people and the affection of children... to appreciate the beauty; to find the best in others; to leave the world a bit better, whether by a healthy child, a garden patch... to know even one life has breathed easier because you have lived. This is to have succeeded!"

Ralph Waldo Emerson

*To read the rest of Dan's story about Ralph Waldo Emerson, please visit www.kathyeldon.com/boundless-extras

YOUR TURN

If you knew you only had six months to live, what would you do?

What's stopping you from doing it now?

CHAPTER 6

ME TO WE–
CONNECTION IS THE SOLUTION

Across the ages, religious leaders have stated that we should "Do unto others as you would have them do unto you." Yet, here we are, juggling sharp-edged words like fiery torches, turning "others" into adversaries over things as trivial as hats and as vast as entire belief systems.

But imagine this: a world where kindness is the currency, where witticisms heal rifts faster than schisms can form, and where humanity collectively says, "Gandhi was right! Let's stop poking each other's eyes out."

This chapter is a call to arms—but not the kind that clangs in battle. No, this is a call to choose to see and be in what may be a braver way for us, challenging us to soften where we've hardened, to reach out where we've withdrawn, and to turn those "others" into the sisters and brothers they've always been. What if, instead of pointing fingers, we offered to hold hands? Instead of tallying hurts, we build bridges.

During existential challenges, we must break free from the stranglehold of division. Let's disarm the "isms" that chain us—racism, tribalism, nationalism—and swap them for the courage to be kind, the audacity to share a funny story, and the bravery to not just dream but to create a boundless way to *see* and *be*.

THIS JOURNEY BEGINS WITH YOU AND ME, AND TOGETHER, WE CAN REBUILD A WORLD WORTH PASSING ON TO THE NOISY, BEAUTIFUL SPIRITS OF TOMORROW.

BRACE YOURSELF

Our earth's pulse is faltering.

For many days before October 7th, 2023,
I could hear a voice
that seemed to whisper in my ear,
Brace yourself, for challenging times lie ahead.
I prepared myself to counter
anything bad I might encounter,
like traffic jams on the I-10,
or oat milk in my latte,
testing my patience yet again.

But that day on my computer screen
I saw scenes that once viewed,
could not be unseen.
From Israel, indelible images of
revelers racing across furrowed fields,
escaping terrorists of Hamas.
By the next morning,
Israel was mourning
over 250 kidnapped, 1100 dead
young and old shot in the head.

Brace yourself, the voice had said,
prepare for challenges that lie ahead.
I breathed in and counted to four,
held my breath and counted four more.
Another breath, then out again,
as reports flowed in of rocket attacks
that left hundreds of Palestinians

wounded or dead,
as life became a living hell
for neighboring nations,
who for generations
have fought and died — for what?

When asked, it seems that most of us
have similar hopes and dreams.
To live in peace with those we love.
To have a safe space to stay,
where kids can run about and play,
near a peaceful place where people can pray.

It's clear that we need to reunite
the people of our planet.
But will it take an alien attack
for us to be friends?
How will it ever end?
Will a comet strike us,
or a pandemic,
worse than before
to remind us there is more
that unites us than keeps us apart,
and that all humankind shares one heart.

Our earth's pulse is faltering.
How gravely wounded,
we know not now.
It's time for humans
to try to be truly kind,
for as Gandhi declared,
an eye for an eye
leaves the whole world blind.

Brace yourself, the voice said.
for challenging times lie ahead.

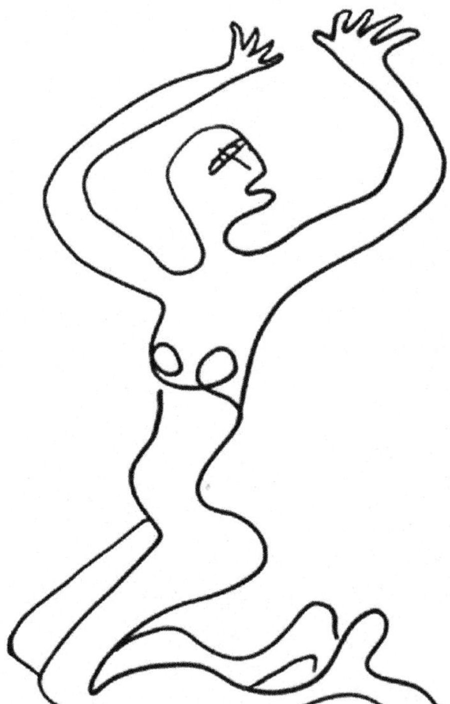

GET IN TROUBLE

I felt fortunate to hear John Lewis speak. With courage, conviction, and humor, he encouraged us all to get in "good trouble."

"Get in the Way,"
John Lewis proclaimed,
"Get in trouble, good trouble," he exclaimed.
That means get out of your bubble,
speak truth to power
and don't let your belief in democracy sour.

Find strength in unity and power in community.
Focus on inequality, injustice,
and the immorality of those
who stand for the rights of the unborn
while turning a blind eye to those they scorn
for being another religion or race,

Bring your brothers and sisters together.
Disturb the status quo wherever you go.
Point to a new destination
for this powerful generation.
Believe you can achieve
all you have been waiting for–
peace, justice, and much, much more.
Never give up, never give in.
Be courageous in all you do,
channeling the powerful energy
flowing through me and through you.

Watch for the glow of John Lewis's star
beaming light through the darkest night.
Although he may seem far away,
you can still hear him say,

*"Get in the way, cause trouble,
good trouble every day."*

YOUR TURN

During the recent fires in LA, I got into "good trouble," I circumvented police barriers to bring food and supplies to those in need. I figured the incredible leader and civil rights activist John Lewis would have been proud of me.

What kind of good trouble can you get up to?

What role can you play in building a more united, compassionate world?

FOR ONE AND FOR ALL

Article One, Section Two of the Constitution of the United States declared that any person who was not free would be counted as three-fifths of a free individual for the purposes of determining congressional representation. Thus, the "Three-Fifths Clause" increased the political power of slaveholding states.

Millions deserve restitution
from the institution that enslaved their kin
when all they craved was the ability
to enjoy the liberty promised in our constitution.
When Jefferson stated that
"all men are created equal,"
he meant only certain people.
Not those who were black,
nor children who were half and half,
fathers betrayed by their offsprings' lightness
and striking likeness to those
who disowned but owned them.

Jefferson is said to have kept
enslaved four of his children
after writing his finest creation,
the revolutionary proclamation
of freedom for his infant.... nation.

Our founding fathers defamed
future generations when
they insanely claimed that
slaves counted as 3/5 of a man,
though they worked more than any human can.

To heal deep wounds caused by
centuries of misuse and abuse
we must rise and devise
a powerful disruption
of this immoral corruption.
Disband and remand vigilantes,
rifles in hand, who scream, "all lives matter,"
as they batter those who march,
hearts filled with sorrow,
hoping for a better tomorrow.

For once and for all, stop rampant racism,
and fight fantastic fascism.
Do all you can to unite the equal people of our land —

FOR ONE-AND FOR ALL.

PURPLE HEART

Soldiers earn a Purple Heart when they are wounded in service. Just think about how great it would be not to have to sacrifice anything but intolerance, bigotry, and hypocrisy to turn our hearts a lovely shade of purple.

Imagine how our country could be
if we focused on the needs of WE,
Instead of just ME, ME, ME.
Instead of being cruel or mean,
let's hold others in esteem,
and team together to build a collective dream.

We all want this country to flourish and to grow,
so, treat strangers as our sisters and our brothers,
seniors as our fathers and our mothers.
Create success for one another
instead of suppressing or oppressing each other.
Be the solution to toxic pollution
caused by those being lewd, crude or rude.
For if humankind is truly kind
we can heal our divided nation.

So, here's an idea of my creation.
Invite your family to a reunion
Then watch for those scared of real union,
standing apart, shielding their hearts
behind armor of red or blue.
Instead of adding more armament
by picking an angry argument,
use love to melt divisive colors
into a more harmonious hue

To save the future of the next generation
let's create a purple-hearted population,
a united nation with no exploitation or condemnation
of red or blue, black or white, they or them, me or you.

BREAKING FREE

It's a joy to watch grandparents who once feared anyone who didn't look like them, proudly embrace their multi-colored grandchildren.

Seventy-two hours is the time
you can confine
those meant
to be demented.
Seventy-two hours
is how long we spent
confined in a mind-set
by those who once sought unity
in a white-flight community.

"Back in the day," they said,
"We fled Blacks and Wops,
Pollacks, Paddies, and Jews,
people of other races, wearing faces
that didn't look like me or you."

Now, their sons and daughters
are marrying those their fathers and mothers
once called the "Others."
Indians, Persians, Mexicans and more.
And now those grandfathers and grandmothers
of multi-colored offspring, daring DNA combinations
from diverse nations say,
"Hey, wake up to a brand-new day.
Break out of mind-confinement
and see how great
a multi-cultural family can be!"

A SWEET SOLUTION

I wrote this the morning after the election when our nation was impossibly divided.

Dear Americans, now that we are through
with the election, let's head a new direction,
release prejudices about each other
and create peace with one another.
Let go of tension.
Create a new intention
to unite, not divide,
aware that unity in community
offers opportunity
for new beginnings,
where winning no longer means
one takes all.
That has been our downfall.
We can do better. And here's how.

Call someone who doesn't think the same as you
and talk about a subject where you can agree,
free of emotion or the silly notion
that one of you must be right.
Keep it light!
Discuss the weather, but not climate change, okay?
Keep that one at bay.
Religion? Not so much.
Hard to keep a light touch.
Football (mmm... tough call,
maybe not such a good idea after all.)

How about sweet treats you both like to eat?
That's a hard subject to beat.
It should be good for a minute or two,
then hang up the phone
before you feel the inclination
to indignantly discuss the state of the nation.
Feel a sense of elation
as you create a new foundation
for a relationship
that can offer kinship
rather than trigger enmity
that could turn you into enemies.

I know we can do it!
But we must commit not to split or quit
for we have only one planet, dammit,
and a tight deadline.
So, instead of maligning each other,
Let's align with one another.
You do your bit, and I'll do mine
and together we will weather this challenging time.

INSANE ISMS

If we listened to ancient wisdom, we could eliminate icky isms.

The Golden Rule for Sikhs and Christians,
Muslims and Jews is, "Do unto others
as you would have them do unto you."
You'll find this rule
in the teachings of most of humankind,
so why don't humans try to be kind
and heed Gandhi's words,
"An eye for an eye and
the whole world becomes blind!"

Starting today,
let's find a brave new way
to SEE and BE.
Let's say "NO" to mean words
that could start a fight
about who's wrong and who's right.
If we stop being demeaning,
driven by envy and greed,
we could be freed
of that which divides
us one from another,
turning those we don't know
into the OTHER.
Instead, let's see them
as our sisters and our brothers,
our fathers and our mothers.

Together, we can stop
Racism, Tribalism, Nationalism and Fascism–

insane isms that cause the world's
most insanely divisive schisms.
Frays and fights,
skirmishes and squabbles,
fallouts and hassles,
Run-in and rows,
tussles and tangles,
vendettas and wrangles
and whacky free-for-alls.
If we bid farewell to nasty spats,
and stop all fights over silly hats.
We can eliminate all icky isms
and heal our world's wounds
with witticisms!

Dear humankind, let's give it a try.
because If humans do unto others
as we would have them do unto us,
things will go better I promise. It's true!
But it all relies on— guess who?

ME and YOU.

PLAYING WITH DNA

CRISPR is a technology used to edit and alter a specific bit of DNA inside a cell.

Now that we can play with DNA,
edit genomes that display
possible cataracts, anemia or cystic fibrosis,
is it possible to cut out neurosis,
narcissism or psychosis?
Eliminate strands that might lead to racism,
or anything that could lead to a schism
between religions, cultures or more?
DNA that could result in war.

Remove pigmentation from our genetic code,
Cafe au lait could be the new mode,
One color for all means no discrimination
Among people in a diverse nation.
CRISPR out sequences that might make us cruel,
Bashing others because we hate a rule.

Apply those molecular scissors
To create more artists, writers and singers,
dancers, lovers and all kinds of givers.
Someone please design a new template for humankind,
A kind human who is color-blind,
but sees with clear vision
a world without division.
Sadly, DNA can't solve our situation
and we can't wait for the next generation,
It's up to us for the re-creation

of who and how we wish to be.
So, if it's not you and me, now,
then who will be, when and how?

THE END OF LIFE AS WE KNEW IT

Little did I know that less than four weeks after writing this little story, the Palisades Fire would destroy my community, leaving nothing but devastation for miles around us. Our house and the Creative Visions Center survived, but Pacific Palisades and Altadena have endured unimaginable losses, leaving them forever changed.

I wanted a vacation,
but not an evacuation,
especially mandatory.
So, here's the story.
It was three in the morning
when a neighbor woke us with a warning.
"Malibu's on fire," he said,
"Get out of bed!"

There was no power,
and at that hour
I was groggy,
our matches were soggy.
With a flashlight in that dark night.
we raced to save valuables,
but what could we choose?
There was so much in our house to lose.

In the end, we chose to stay,
watching neighbors as they sped away,
while smoke and soot from flames cresting the hills
choked our throats and gave us chills.

For the next three days,
we were on a cold, dark staycation

with too much time to think,
about how, in a blink,
floods and fires,
tornadoes, cyclones, hurricanes,
effects of man-made climate change,
have changed our lives forever.
Even if humans change
there'll be no return to life as we knew it.
Never. Ever.

THIS IS YOUR MOTHER SPEAKING

A reminder that we humans are well past our sell-by date.

Do you even see what you're doing to me?
I give you everything, and you just take, take, take
without realizing the sacrifices I make.
Unaware of how to care, much less to share.
You ask why my temperature is rising.
Well, it's easy to explain. I'm feeling overheated
and defeated by who and how you are.
This unkind treatment has gone too far.

I am your mother, after all, not some random other.
I am the air. The land. The sea. All are me.
You are the child of this we.
Two of the three breaths you take are from the air I make.
I spawned you and all living creatures from my womb
but when I watch you looking at me,
I know that I'm doomed.

I see your superficial gaze,
but perhaps your vision is blurred by the haze
of smoke from forests ablaze
leaving no safe space, no hidden place
from infernos, which rage and rage.
You say you love me.
So why do you use and abuse me,
capture my treasures without measure
leak oil, dump chemicals, and worse,
Honestly, my child, I hate to say it,
but I see you as a curse.
You poison my oceans, bleach coral reefs

Hook, snare, net innocent creatures deep beneath.
Apparently, you believe I'll be able to recreate
what has taken millennia to procreate.

Clearly this is not working for me, nor for you.
Remember, as I gave you breath,
I shall be responsible for your death.
So, stop being reckless
with the one you should love.
Give more to me than you receive.
Say no to what you don't need,
sparkly objects born of greed.
Don't be deceived and believe there
are other sources for my precious resources.
When my land is parched, and my sky is gray
with ash and soot from fires that have burned away
my grasses and flowers, trees and more,
there will be worse pain for you in store.

For my sea too will be free of life
save formless shapes in the deep recesses
of my hidden crevices,
ready to make a quiet entrance,
millennia from now.
New life begun in my deep womb
will emerge again to dispel earth's gloom.
Swim first with newly webbed feet,
then walk on land, a remarkable feat.
From then, we know that wings will grow
and in the clear blue skies of tomorrow,
I shall finally forget my sorrow.
Seeing creatures live in peace and safely grow
will quell my pain, I know,

but if they, like you, descend into greed
use more than they need,
then they too, will have to go.

So please heed my warning
and awaken to a brand-new morning
sparked by mourning for all you have lost.
Treat me as your loving mother,
and let's work with one another.
We, the land, the sea–you and me entwined,
together can save all humankind.
But, hurry, please, for you must appreciate
that very soon, it will be too late,
as you, my child, are past your sell-by date.

YOUR TURN

If you were Mother Earth, what would be your message to humanity?

Write a short letter sharing your hopes, concerns, and what you wish humans would change.

A NEW CREATION

Five months into the Covid shutdown, I awakened in the middle of the night with this poem flowing through me. It was the first and most important message my Noisy Spirits transmitted to me.

Imagine a nation
a new creation
united in peace and love

Imagine a nation
our creation,
disruption dispelling corruption
igniting positive change

Imagine the world as this nation.
Community powering unity
over time and space.
Imagine this unity
sparking opportunity
across generations and race

Imagine this nation
a new creation
bringing joy and grace

Imagine this nation
imagine it now.
Our creation.
Our nation.

So what's *your* part–and how?

A STORY TO MAKE YOU FEEL BETTER ABOUT LIFE, LOVE AND THE FUTURE OF HUMANITY

I wanted to ask someone famous to wrap up this book, but when I reached out to my Noisy Spirits, it seemed they wanted to have the last word. I was delighted when they told me that former United Nations Secretary General, U Thant, had organized a roundtable to discuss what they should say and invited me to join them. Please note that I did my best to take down everyone's comments, but it was a bit hectic with all those flapping wings and clanking halos.

The Secretary General tapped on a glass to get everyone's attention. "The war we have to wage today has only one goal and that is to make the world safe for diversity," he stated.

Chief Seattle took a long puff on his pipe. Plumes of smoke swirled around him as he began to speak. "All things are bound together. All things connect. All things share the same breath–the beast, the tree, the man... the air shares its spirit with all the life it supports. Man does not weave this web of life. He is merely a strand of it. Whatever he does to the web, he does to himself."

When he had finished everyone sat quietly for a moment. President Kennedy broke the silence, saying that he agreed with the Chief, but wondered what people, once they had connected with each other, should do to ensure that the planet would survive. "Things do not happen, they are made to happen," he declared.

Suddenly all hell broke loose (which I thought was quite inappropriate given where we were). It seemed that everyone had a different idea about how to approach the challenges we face. It got really noisy until my son Dan dove into the conversation. "Seek solutions, not problems," he shouted over the din.

You could hear a pin drop. I was proud when Ruth Bader Ginsberg flashed a smile at Dan, then drew herself to her full height of 5'1", "You can disagree without being disagreeable," she said, glaring over her glasses. "Fight for the things that you care about but do it in a way that will lead others to join you."

Mahatma Gandhi explained what he thought was important. "A nation's culture lies in the hearts and souls of its people," he said. His words struck a chord as the spirits literally rose from their chairs. Ralph Waldo Emerson, wearing his Great American Scholar leather jacket, climbed onto the table before crying out, "The one thing in the world of value is the active soul, free, sovereign, unencumbered... this every man holds within, but in most it's obstructed and as yet unborn."

There were loud cheers from the crowd. I raised my hand, but no one took any notice. The Secretary General had to shush everyone before I could speak. "I love the idea of an activated soul," I said, "but once souls are awakened, what should they do?"

Mother Teresa raised her hand. "Just respond to people's needs," she said, her voice sounding surprisingly strong for such a tiny person. Then I remembered what Bishop Desmond Tutu, surely an angel with skin, once said, "Do a little bit of good wherever you are; it's those bits of good that will overwhelm the planet."

Suddenly, Teddy Roosevelt sprang to his feet, "Do what you can with what you have where you are!" he shouted, slashing the air with his sword. Giving him a look, Eleanor Roosevelt rose and declared, in her dignified way, "You must do the thing you think you cannot do."

Very inspiring, I thought, but there is SO much we have to do to sort out our world. Sir Winston Churchill must have noticed my anxiety. Blowing cigar smoke my way, he launched into a tirade, "Bloody well keep calm and carry on, woman. Everyday you may make progress. Yet there will stretch out before you an ever-lengthening, ever-ascending, ever-improving path. You know you will never get to the end of the journey. But this, so far from discouraging, only adds to the joy and glory of the climb."

"It always seems impossible until it's done," Nelson Mandela said reassuringly.

Then someone pulled out a harp and another, a harmonica. Soon everyone was clapping and singing. I loved that Nelson Mandela invited Mother Teresa and Ruth Bader Ginsberg to join him in an impromptu conga dance. Dan stood with me as they twirled around the room. "Thanks for listening, Mum," he said, his eyes sparkling. "We've waited a long time to get through to you and all the other earth people who have been screwing up the planet. You can restore balance again, but you have to get going. There's very little time left. You'll have to be very creative and work fast."

My eyes welled as I realized that it was time for me to leave. "Always remember that I love you," Dan said, hugging me so tightly I could barely breathe.

Seeing the tears streaming down my face, Maya Angelou enveloped us both in her arms. "Love recognizes no barriers," she whispered, "It jumps hurdles, leaps fences, penetrates walls to arrive at its destination full of hope." Hope. That word again.

Dan smiled as he shook his head. "Remember, Miss Angelou, the Journey is the Destination."

Reluctantly, I said goodbye to them and tiptoed out of the room. Stepping into the night, I was surprised to hear Martin Luther King call after me, "Only in the darkness can you see the stars."

I looked up. To my surprise, Bob Marley was hovering right in front of me. "Everything's gonna be alright!" He said with a cheeky grin. I held open the door for him as he swooped down to join the noisy flutter of spirits inside.

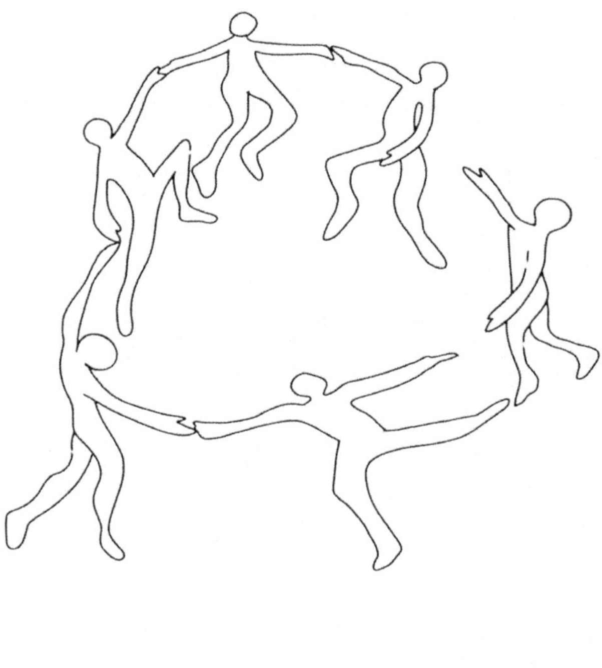

As we ask existential questions about our future, we must remind ourselves that despite all the difficult times we have endured over time, the human spirit, although beaten down, shattered, and battered, has always endeavored to rise, to find new hope, to grow and expand, seeking solutions to the problems we face.

If we respond to the "blessed unrest" that Martha Graham describes as within us, we will find the resilience and strength to see and manifest the solutions we find into a new reality. But it will require us to go from ME to WE.

Connected to one another, we can–and must–transform our collective pain into a powerful, positive force for good.

I know we can do it.

YOUR TURN

What are your dreams for your future?

What are your dreams for the future of the world?

So, what's your part and how?

YOUR INNER COMPASS: *The S.P.A.R.K.*

I promised you "a roadmap to a limitless future"—but in truth, you are the only one who can create a map for your life. To spark your imagination, I have shared my own journey, a long and winding road that initially felt beyond my ability to navigate without a map. But through the ups and downs and in-betweens, I discovered a compass. It's not the usual one we hold in our hands, but a compass that lives deep within—ignited by a SPARK that no one else can see or measure. It's the flicker that wakes you up and says *there's more*; it's the fire within you that, once fanned, illuminates a future where the obstacles you face are opportunities to find a new direction.

The original spark for my compass was my STORY, raw, real, and wildly mine, but a story I knew I had to change. To find my way out of the *Waiting Game,* I created my S.P.A.R.K. compass and used it to embark on a journey that has challenged every aspect of my being, but taught me to eagerly anticipate the adventures that lie ahead. That inner compass has helped me continue to find a new direction and rewrite my story.

Now, if you wish, I am inviting you to rewrite your story.

As you prepare to break free from your *Box called Me,* it's time to reconnect with your PURPOSE. Remember, our purpose is not handed to us, but discovered over and over through reflection, curiosity, and deep listening to what your soul came here to do. So, now is the time to be still and listen inside to your Noisy Spirits, Muses, Quantum Energy, The Universe/Source/God – or simply put, your intuition.

When you start living on purpose, it's time to ACTIVATE—to engage with the world, however you define it. Embrace your journey, not as a fixed route with a defined destination, but as an unfolding adventure of *Becoming* who you really are. Activating your soul gives you the courage to keep going, even if the path is unclear.

When the terrain gets tough (and it will), you must call on your RESILIENCE. Not as a stiff, brittle demeanor, but as a way of seeing and being that understands when it's time to rest and re-center, and when it's the moment to rise again, stronger and more open than before. You'll need all the resilience you can muster to deal with the challenges of *Love. Lost. Love Found.* The despair that comes with *Life. Death. Life.* of those we cherish is crushing, though the prospect of the human spirit enduring fuels our energy as we move forward.

Through it all, let KINDNESS be your true north, both toward yourself and others. Let it guide your thoughts, your actions, and your voice. Because the most boundless lives are not lived alone. Living from *Me to We* means that our energy ripples outward, touching everything and everyone with compassion and light.

So hold your compass close. Let it activate your spirit. Let it help you rewrite the story you thought you had to live. Then go—boldly, joyfully, imperfectly—into the wild, beautiful unknown.

At the beginning of this book, I told you how my 21-year-old son, Dan, photographed images that helped trigger "Operation Restore Hope," a global aid mission that saved the lives of hundreds of thousands of starving Somalis. But I didn't tell you how he got there. At 14, Dan organized a "Save a Heart" initiative to raise funds for a young Kenyan classmate to have a heart operation. Two years later, he rallied his school to buy beaded jewelry from his Masai "mother" to support her children. At 19, Dan invited his friends to travel across Africa in two Land Rovers to bring essential aid to a refugee camp in Malawi. Dan started by helping one person, then a family, next a community, and finally a country.

When my son was killed at the age of 22, we thought his spark had been extinguished forever. But, at his "Celebration of Life" in Nairobi, his friends lit a fire with flaming torches, saying, "This is to commemorate the sparks Dan lit in others."

I am joyous, realizing how much good trouble Dan's boundless spark has inspired. His vibrant spirit continues to encourage countless others to believe they, too, can have a role to play in changing the world around them for the better.

Now I invite you to find the SPARK compass within you as you embark on your own limitless journey. And remember, you can't get lost, because, as Dan said:

THE JOURNEY IS THE DESTINATION

YOUR TURN

My S.P.A.R.K. compass has guided me. You can use my words–STORY, PURPOSE, ACTIVATE, RESILIENCE and KINDNESS, or choose others for your compass that more closely align with where you are on your journey. Remember that every chapter of your life, especially the messy ones, have prepared you to move forward with greater empathy, insight, and strength.

YOUR BOUNDLESS LIFE BEGINS NOW

ENDINGS AND BEGINNINGS

We are at the end of this book, but not the end of the journey. I hope that *Boundless* might just be the beginning—a nudge, a wink, a kick in the pants– to remind us that there's always more to see, more to be, and more to experience, even if you're not quite sure how.

At the heart of *Boundless* lies a profound invitation to live fully, to look deeply, and to embrace the beauty of both being and seeing in a way that opens up limitless new opportunities and possibilities to transform ourselves and the world around us. Through these pages, we have explored fragments of life that are, at once, deeply personal yet wholly universal and, I hope, may touch something true in all of us.

Perhaps the stories I have shared can act as markers on a journey through life's chaos and beauty, reminding us of our shared humanity and of the bravery it takes to keep our hearts open in a world that is constantly shifting. Amy and I were profoundly challenged not to shut down our hearts after Dan's death–but, rather, to try to transform his death into a force for good. At first, we were totally broken - and completely broke. We questioned whether we could make any kind of impact at all. When we started Creative Visions Foundation in my two-bedroom condo in West Hollywood nearly three decades ago, we had no idea that Dan's legacy would illuminate a brave new path forward for countless individuals across the planet.

Never in my wildest dreams could I have imagined that Creative Visions would incubate hundreds of creative activist projects and productions globally, touching more than 100 million people, nor that our youth empowerment programs would inspire generations of young people to believe they had a role in changing the world around them through creative expression. Now I know that almost anything is possible, but first, you must have a dream, a vision– a spark, fueled by your life force, your vitality and stirred by the "blessed unrest" you feel within. I wonder what good trouble you can get into in your home, your neighborhood and your community with your creative spark? What ripples of hope can you launch in your state, your country and our world?

Remember, being boundless doesn't mean being perfect—it means being brave enough to show up, try again, and let yourself find ways to expand beyond the limits that confine you. Even if you can't leave your home, you can embrace a new way of seeing and being that will change your life. There is courage in this kind of being, one that seeks possibility in every moment, no matter how imperfect.

May these words remind you that you are never alone on your journey. Whether you are beginning again, holding a light for others, or gathering the energy to face what's next, you are part of something larger, an unstoppable global movement of individuals who believe in a better world, one that offers hope and limitless new opportunities for positive transformation, inside and out.

Sending you much love on your journey,

Kathy Eldon

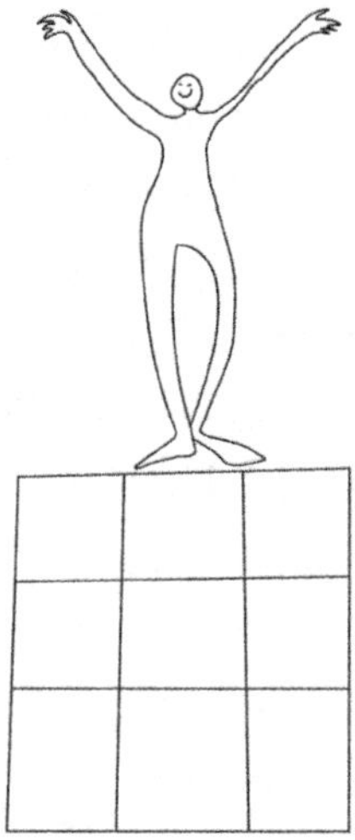

GET INVOLVED

Boundless author Kathy Eldon is a best-selling author, award-winning film producer, and the founder of Creative Visions Foundation and Creative Visions Productions, which has produced award-winning feature films, documentaries, a PBS series and an animated film, *Harper's Yellow Goggles*. Kathy's 18 books include her memoir, *In the Heart of Life*, and the popular *Catcher* guided journal series written with her daughter Amy. Kathy's son, Reuters photojournalist Dan Eldon, killed while on assignment in Somalia, is the inspiration for *The Journey is the Destination*, a feature film based on his journals. To learn more about Kathy Eldon, her work or invite her to speak, please visit www.kathyeldon.com.

Creative Visions is a United Nations Non-governmental organization founded by Kathy and Amy in 1998 to celebrate Dan Eldon's life. Since then, Creative Visions has touched the lives of more than 100 million people. To learn more about Creative Visions, please visit www.creativevisions.org.

To learn more about Dan Eldon's life and legacy, or purchase fine art prints of his journal pages, please visit www.daneldoncollection.com.

Additional books to explore:

In the Heart of Life
Angel Catcher: A Journal of Loss and Remembrance
Angel Catcher for Kids: A Journal to Help You Remember the Person You Love Who Died
Soul Catcher: A Journal to Help You Become Who You Really Are
Love Catcher: Inviting Love Into Your Life
The Journey is the Destination: The Journals of Dan Eldon
The Journey is the Destination: Artist's Journal
Safari as a Way of Life
Dan Eldon: The Art of Life
Tastes of Kenya
Safari Diary
Making Music in Kenya
Eating Out in Kenya
Specialities of the House from Kenya's Finest Restaurants
Kitchens and Cooking
The Story of Medicine
Tom-tom to Television

ACKNOWLEDGEMENTS

With deep gratitude to my Noisy Spirits (with skin) who helped manifest *Boundless*. All thanks to Managing Editor Alicia Dougherty and Creative Director Tihane, without whom absolutely nothing. I'm grateful to Andi Gitow for her editorial genius, and to our brilliant production team including editor Rachel Warmath, and graphic designers Hillary Mix, Kyle Hollingsworth and EJ Phillips. My heartfelt thanks go to readers Mary Anne Fitzgerald, Dianne Gray, John Wellso, Amy St. Onge and Elizabeth Morris for their support of this project.

Thank you to my invisible team of Noisy Spirits led by my son, Dan Eldon, with back-up from my parents, Russell and Louise Knapp and dearest friends, Donald Ranvaud, and Adrian House. A most special thanks to my extraordinary daughter, Amy Eldon Turteltaub, my boundless mentor Eva Haller, my always-supportive husband, Michael Bedner, and limitless Creative Visions CEO, Pat Chandler, who encouraged me to be brave and get this book out of my mind and into the world.

YOUR TURN

Printed in Dunstable, United Kingdom

65164204R00097